Together we

Benedict O'Boyle

Mud, Sweat and Tear Gas

Volunteering in the Calais Jungle

Benedict O'Boyle

insight2foresight publishing

6 Burton Close

Wheathampstead

AL4 8LU

United Kingdom

Email: info@i2fpublishing.co.uk

First published 2016 © Benedict O'Boyle

The right of Benedict O'Boyle to be identified as the author of this work has been asserted by him in accordance with the Copyright, Designs and Patents Act of 1998

Photographs are copyright of Beatrice Lily Lorigan ©2016

ISBN 978-1-909345-15-7

British Library Cataloguing-in-Publication Data

A catalogue record for this book is available from the British Library

Acknowledgements

Thank you from the refugees to all of you who have made donations. Thank you Christina for the repeated horse van loans.

One love and thanks to the amazing family of volunteers, who have restored my faith in humanity by achieving the impossible time after time and become my friends.

A huge thank you, to my wife Anya and daughter Layla, for you continued patience, compassion and support, despite my absences and the challenge of repeatedly moving between very different worlds. Thanks also to Beatrice Lily Lorigan for the images, (Aunty) Linda O'Boyle and (Mum) Sue O'Boyle for the help editing my ramblings.

Most of all thank you to the refugees, who welcomed me, shared what little they had, and showed unimaginable courage and character, as we shared innumerable cups of tea.

Dedication

This book is dedicated to the amazing refugees of the Calais Jungle, it has been my honour, thank you for the love, the laughter and the tea. See you in UK.

Foreword by Leon Aarts. Building Bridges

An old African saying says: 'In a time of floods we build bridges.' That is exactly what Ben has done since he started to visit the refugee and migrant camps in and around Calais. The UK only really became aware of the "Jungle' in Calais in September 2015 when Aryan Kurdi was found dead on a beach in Greece.

Suddenly it hit home that there was a huge stream of people migrating to Europe, all trying to find a safe and peaceful place to live. The press informed us that there was a camp with about 6000 people at the time living right on our doorstep. Most British and European citizens panicked and went into fear, fear which was deepened by our politicians and the media telling us that the people living in the camps who were desperate, homeless, torn, hurt, abused and bombed upon, were only here to take our wealth, money and resources.

A tactic which has been used numerous times over the centuries to influence us, and which is now so refined now and steeped into our culture that most people believe it. It didn't stop a few souls who knew that we couldn't let these people suffer, that we needed to do whatever we could.

Ben was one of them, he saw our common humanity, that connection which binds us all, that we are all human beings deserving equal rights and value. Or as Ben would say in his own words; 'to treat others how you want to be treated.' A steady stream of hundreds of volunteers filled their cars and vans with aid, giving their time, money and resources. Later this movement became thousands, going from Calais to as far as the Greek Isles, Turkey and Syria.

It was a huge undercurrent, a flow which no-one saw coming, just as most people were surprised when they heard about the millions of refugees fleeing their homes mainly because of the actions of the *western world bombing their homes, funding rogue prime ministers or giving arms and ammunition to terrorists. Dividing us and hiding what it all was really about.*

This undercurrent of people, human beings with their heart in the right place, started to do what they thought was needed, using their skills, imagination and resources. None of the large aid and human rights organisations were present as of course the whole crisis was too political,. They were afraid to lose their funding from the governments, the same governments who just claimed these people fleeing, war are terrorists and illegal. How can any human being ever be illegal?

This large movement of people connected, became self organised and magically everything got done. Food was brought to the camps, clothes, tents, doctors came, a theatre and women centre. When we connect to something which is bigger than us, magic truly happens… What is bigger, is to look each other in the eye and to see and realise our common humanity. All the people I have met in my time helping in the camps, that is what connected each and everyone of us. That not just gives hope, these connections ensure that things get done. That we are there for each other regardless our religion, colour, background, education or nationality. It doesn't matter for what reason someone decides to leave their friends, family and home behind, that is not relevant. They are people in need and we can help. What is relevant is that they felt they had too, a step which is not easily taken. Imagine it just could have been us…..

I met Ben in December when he first came to camp, he wanted to help and used his skills in the building team to build huts, shelters, people's homes, places where they live, sleep, can find a moment of peace and security for themselves and most importantly be dry and warm.

When Ben started to share his stories with us on Facebook, many of us were struck by the way he wrote about the people he met, never judging, always understanding, seeing them as human beings. Working relentlessly when he was in the camps, whilst having a young family and business at home, showing us what really can be achieved when we come together and connect with our hearts.

Make no mistake about, as he writes lightly the circumstances where often difficult, not just the rain, wind and cold weather but the pressure cooker in which the residents have been living often for many years brought many difficult situations and tension. The 20 or so different nationalities living close to each other with hardly any protection, the constant interrogation and abuse by the CRS, the French riot police. The unknown future, the despair and little hope, Ben turns it all in a beautiful story of humanity. We as westerners can learn so much from these people, the dignity with which they live, the love and gratitude they show.

Unfortunately I have to say they don't receive the same from our Western society.

One of the biggest challenges for each and everyone of us is the feeling of not being heard or seen, or being taken for granted. That is often more difficult than the actual situation you find yourself in. We label human beings as illegal, gold diggers, we put them in camps behind barbed wire and deploy a huge army of fully armed riot police who talk with tear-gas and rubber bullets to fight off their own boredom.

Ben gives the people a voice and sees them as equal. That is the beauty of this book and I highly recommend you to read and share it with your friends and family. It is a great discussion starter, to create what Ben and myself would love: A more beautiful world, a world in which everyone is treated equally and has the same chances.

Leon Aarts Founder of #Istand and Calais Kitchens, feeding thousands in and around Calais

"Together we are change"

I had read the post online: "A call for help! Carpenters, with the skills to build shelters for refugees in Calais." I had found the line; it had already been crossed.

I couldn't sit at home and complain any longer; screaming out into social media and expecting some sort of revolution to occur. I couldn't listen to the media paint the picture of terrorists and scroungers, banging on our door; people to be feared. They were just people fleeing violence. I couldn't read about children in tents anymore and be outraged. What right did I have to be outraged? I knew better than to expect my government to do anything to help. It had become alarmingly clear, they would do nothing and people would die.

Winter was coming and it was down to the people to help...and I was people. I could help, maybe make a difference and maybe even find out the truths behind the stories: The Truths of the Calais Jungle.

Disclaimer

I'm too busy to take many photos and it's a sensitive matter. I'm not a volunteer having a look and taking a selfie for my online profile. I'm there to work hard and help people. Whilst there is a need for images of the jungle, it's not my role to take them. Because of this I try to paint the best picture I can with my words. Thank you for your patience. Here goes:

The Workshop:

Albert, a local friend, and I left at 2am, collected donations en route and 'chunneled' to Calais for the 9am briefing.

We arrived at an abandoned industrial estate and were shown a warehouse with a kitchen that provided volunteers with a hot lunch and organised food donations and distribution. A mountain of bin bags full of stupid donations at the front, sold by the ton, and recycled.

At the back was the sorting area, bustling with people sorting everything from medicines, tents, tarpaulins, clothes, toys and more. We unloaded our donations. The tools in the back gave away our skill set, so despite being exhausted, we headed straight to the workshop and started making shelter frames from 2"x2" pine. We got set up and cracked on.

We worked until 9pm alongside various teams, making various parts, like wrapping doors in tarpaulins, cutting timber to length or whatever needed doing. Anyone who could use a saw and a drill could do this work. We made a lot of frames and talked to a few people about the situation. Van drivers would come in and collect the shelter components and nails/screws required to build them and ferry them back and forth to the build crews in the Jungle.

We spoke to a few people, but mainly worked. We listened to accounts of 'The Jungle' as it was known by refugees and volunteers alike. There was a lot of positivity but obvious pain; fighting a losing battle against weather, funding, volunteers and materials, whilst more refugees arrived every day and over 8000 people were living in sodden tents in a filthy hell-hole.

We set up the pop up tent in the back of the van, had a few beers and went to bed, exhausted but feeling positive.

The Jungle:

I arrived in the workshop ready to make more frames, but overhear a build crew saying they could do with another pair of hands building shelters on site. Before I knew it, I was driving to the camp with Tom and Glen and a load of tools.

As I pulled off the motorway, passing the flashing blue lights and angry looking French CRS police. I could see across the sprawl of The Jungle and finally appreciated the size of the problem. Thousands of tired tents, tarpaulin shelters and makeshift buildings peppered the muddy field all were interspersed with litter. It was a horrendous mess.

I parked at the entrance, as we unloaded the van, inquisitive refugees keeping an eye on the motorway trucks, gathered in an orderly queue and asked, "Line? Line?"

"No line my friends, we are here to build shelters," Tom informed them. They understood and appreciated that we were there to help and returned to their business of watching and waiting.

We lugged our tools into the camp, past the toilets, with the stench of human waste stinging my nose and eyes. Ignoring the wet mud, we walked through the Afghan area, past little shanty-town shops selling food and drink from makeshift shelters and small restaurants serving great looking food.

People were singing, smiling and laughing, holding onto their dignity as their world disintegrated into fear and filth. A few had their faces covered by scarves and their angry eyes burned with fury as we passed. Their dislike for the Westerners whose governments had a hand in destroying their lives and killing their loved ones was clear, and I could not blame them.

We trudged on past water points, distribution centres, the brothel and the church.

Eventually we made it to the Women's and children's area, a safe haven created to protect from the horrors that had befallen most of the vulnerable. We delivered and installed a projector and then headed back out to see whom we could help.

There was no shortage of people who needed us. I had brought some tarpaulins, which we used to waterproof a few tents and shelters, the mud and conditions generally making progress slow. Everywhere we went people would ask for help.

"Hello, one minute please sir, you help?" Five minutes later, they had a fixed door latch, or some nails to hang clothes from or a verbal agreement that we would try and get them a shelter.

Nothing takes a minute in the jungle and everyone needs help. Every time we fixed something, another person would come over and ask for help. We were shown small leaky tents that housed 8 people, whether it was a waterproof roof, a repaired lock, or just giving them some nails. They were always grateful and often invited us for tea. But at this point I felt that there was too much to do for a tea break. So we worked on.

By the time we headed back to the van with our tools at 8pm, it had been dark for a while. I was covered in mud from the knees down, and still trying to process the humanity alongside the inhumane conditions.

The Jungle was beginning to wake up for the night. The atmosphere changing as music came blaring out of a large, black plastic covered building: The Sudanese Bar/night club with the hustle and bustle of people emerging from their tents to eat or socialise.

We didn't see any trouble, but did feel the potential bubbling under the surface; only a spark would be needed for an explosion of anger or frustration. The suffering these people had endured to get this far had left many irreparably damaged. They try to get along, despite the conditions, their journey and being such a wide demographic of people- Afghani, Eritreans, Kurdish, Pakistani, Iranian, Iraqi, Syrian, Sudanese and many more. Nations that previously disliked each other, now forced together in abhorrent conditions, while striving for a peaceful life in a living hell. They ran from bombs and death, hoping for a safer life, but almost all have lost loved ones and now all they have is hope.

My initial social media post:

The Jungle, is an amazingly diverse community of refugees arriving overland from various countries in the Middle East and Africa, trying to coexist and survive as best as is humanly possible. There is laughter and music and song. The mud is like Glastonbury... in December, after a year of chaos. There are: broken tents and plastic clad pine shelters everywhere; shops and shanty restaurants, mud, more mud and then mud. But the people on the whole are lovely; they appreciate the help and regularly ask, "What will the British Government do to help us? Is there hope?"

I don't know the answer; I don't believe our Government will do enough to help the displaced citizens of the countries they are destroying. But I have to look them in the eye and say, "There is always hope."

In the morning, we made some bunk beds and installed them, did running repairs on shelters and agreed to find a base for 9 people who were on the ground in a tent. We will take them a base tomorrow. We then spoke to people who needed a new roof, which we will fit tomorrow. They have lashed tree branches together and the water pools in the plastic sheeting and it leaks. They have to keep pushing the roof up during the night to stop it leaking and if it snows it will collapse.

We ate dinner in the Afghan Flag restaurant: amazing food, lovely people fighting to create a community and keep going, despite the abhorrent conditions.

The volunteers are amazing, doing so much with so little. Some have been here months and just can't bring themselves to leave. I know how they feel.

For the first time in a long time, I cried tonight. I love you all.

As people here say, "It is what it is."

A long day:

We loaded the horse van with supplies to fix a roof and headed to the jungle, refugees now recognising us as familiar faces.

A teenager approached and asked, "I help you brother?"

We tell him where we are going (it may take him out of his territory and place him in danger), he shrugs so I hand him some timber to carry and loaded with tools and materials we trudge on through the mud.

We arrive at the shelter and are greeted like old friends. The eldest, Mohammed, an Economics professor, put a pot of water for tea straight onto the small gas hob.

They clear their 3.5m2 shelter, piling all their belongings into the corner. We put down plastic to protect their home from the mud and start cutting the string that lashed together the branches.

Nasser, who is in his early twenties, speaks excellent English and studied Mathematics helps, passing the branches out as we remove and support the roof. The branches are cut up for firewood, which is always needed in the jungle.

We stop for tea and have a chat with our hosts. Familiar, sad stories of loss and pain are mixed with jokes and laughing. Mohammed tells me all he has is hope and Nasser asks if I can help him get to England. "I will be your servant forever my brother," he pleads.

"If I can get you to England my brother then you will be my friend forever," I reply. We talk about our governments. I apologise for our countries role in their tragedy.

Mohammed smiles and says, "We have a government too. They don't listen to their people."

⌘

The roof takes a few hours, but by the time we are done he has 2"x2" timber rafters, with 50mm Celotex insulation, I brought over with me. It's sloped and sturdy and won't collapse if it snows. Glen hangs from the roof to show its strength and jokes about his weight;

we all laugh. We have a coffee as we tidy up, ready for the next job and I take Nasser's number and give him mine.

"I will do what I can." I promise him.

Knowing they will be warm, dry and safe now, they are all in high spirits. I'm invited back for dinner, but have to decline, as I'm the driver.

"Tomorrow night my brother, please let us cook for you."

I explain that there are so many brothers that need our help I may not be able to, but agree to try and promise to at least return for tea before I leave. There are warm hugs for all as we leave and Mohammed kisses my cheek with tears in his eyes and thanks me again. I tell him to keep looking after the lads he's with and to keep

hope. With mixed emotions, we load up and hike on to the next site, knowing we have made a difference, but barely.

Before we left France, I kept my promise and returned to see my friends for tea and biscuits.

⌘

The next site is a medium sized tepee style tent. It's right on the edge of the 'road'.

There are 8 people sleeping in it and the floor is always wet as it is sat on mud. They have been living like that for months.

I put my head in the shower block next door, a set up run by Amir. He is from Pakistan and speaks eight languages. Amir organises the lads in the tent and we lay a tarpaulin out on the floor for their damp belongings. Amir is living between the Sudanese and the Iranians, having moved out of the Afghan area to avoid the trouble making. I used his skills numerous times in the jungle and he was always happy to help his brothers of any nationality.

I've managed to scavenge two bases, left over from heavier duty shelters they used to make. With difficulty, we unload them from the lorry. One gets caught and then gives, suddenly sliding and smashing me in the face. We remove the tent and flatten the ground with a shovel, before screwing the bases together. There are smiles all round as we re-erect the tent and they know they will be dry tonight.

Our next job is to put up a shelter with some teenagers who have been on the list for a month, but as we prepare to leave an angry Iranian man in his 60's is shouting at me, gesticulating with tears running down his face.

I fetch Amir and he translates. The man is camped next to the road, which is a mud track with huge puddles. Every time a vehicle passes, filthy water washes into his tent. I look inside and there is 2" of muddy water in there. It smells of sewage. The man is distressed because he knows they will die if they sleep there and there is nowhere else to go. But they are only 4 adult men and have no hope of getting a shelter.

I tell Amir I will be back shortly. The angry man shouts at me, believing that I won't return, but Amir tells him I am a good man and to have faith.

I track down Pete, the van driver, and ask about a shelter. I explain the situation and Pete tells us to take the last two shelters in the van, he'll head back and get some more.

We split our build team and Glen and I return to Amir with the lorry, after dropping the others to build elsewhere. It's late afternoon and the temperature is dropping. It's been an hour since I left, but getting around and finding people in The Jungle is difficult and you have to surrender to "Jungle time".

Amir scolds the angry man and enjoys his moment of being right. The angry man bows his head and touches his chest. I smile and give him a hug and tell him he will be dry tonight.

⌘

The shelters take a few hours to unload, assemble, clad with plastic and insulate, the ground is rarely level or flat. It's dark by the time we finish and our drill batteries are almost as tired as us. The guys helped where they could: holding timber or stapling plastic sheeting down. They are very careful and know this may be their home for a while.

It's about 8pm by the time we say our goodbyes, meet up with the others and head to the van. Someone runs past us splashing through the mud, and then another and another. This is unusual, people don't run in the jungle; it's slippery and messy and nobody wants to get injured. Within a few seconds there are hundreds of people running and cheering excitedly towards the entrance of the camp and the van. We hear that there is a traffic jam on the highway and the trucks have stopped! Everyone is running to try and jump on one before they move again.

Glen and I agree this is a desperate side of the situation and we don't want to see, people potentially risking their lives to escape. We are not here for entertainment.

We head back into the jungle and go to the Sudanese pub for a beer, glad to sit down. As we drink our beer we hear the, "Pop, pop," of a grenade launcher and people running and shouting. The police have started firing tear gas into the camp. We can smell and taste it, and even inside the tent our eyes were stinging. Outside, people near the chemical weapons being used would be blinded temporarily and in a lot of pain. We finish our beers, thank and pay our hosts. It has returned to normal again outside: people eating and laughing, singing and smiling.

We get back to the van, which would have had a prime view of the earlier melee, but it's calm now and we finally head off.

You could do it too:

We met Josh and Marcus at the workshop, they'd been making shelter components for days and were ready to go into the jungle and help assembly. We jumped in the van and headed in. The more the merrier.

I watched their expressions of horror and sadness as they took in the sight of The Jungle sprawl, a canvas of tents and mud, as we made our way past the overflowing toilets near the entrance. As we walked past the shops and restaurants and made our way deeper in, I tried to answer the same questions I myself had asked only days ago. I had learned so much and most of my fears and queries had been satiated, but to think I was now considered informed was a worry. The Jungle is a complex and dangerous place, beautiful and terrible all at once.

Marcus, a big guy, with long dreads and always a smile, quickly found himself at ease, with lots of nods and 'hello brothers' from the passing refugees. I saw his eyes start to change from sadness, as the singing and smiling sparked back the glimmer of hope, and the initial horror subsided. If you can sing in a place like this then there is hope.

The group we were assembling the shelter for were pretty helpful, holding timbers for sawing and helping wrap the plastic sheeting as taut as possible. The usual difficulty of, "Where is my shelter," and, "Please, one minute you fix," from other groups nearby makes Jungle time slip by, as we pop to fix a lock or staple a tarpaulin.

But we work hard and have a couple of shelters up in time for a late lunch. We meet up with the others and head to eat. The first restaurant is out of food. We came too late. The next gives us the thumbs up and we sit and eat. It's good to rest and talk to like-minded people, plus the food is excellent.

After feeding body and soul, we all make more shelters in the afternoon. I pop into the women's and children's area, to deliver a snow-suit and call in at the kids' centre as I pass, to confirm a rumour: The cot bed I made has been smashed up by a young boy. It can't be repaired, but the mattress is at least still usable. I ask about the boy; he is 7 and is here alone. He doesn't know if his parents are alive and, after his harrowing journey, he had been abused since his arrival.

Although systems are now in place to protect the vulnerable, The Jungle is still dangerous for a child. I didn't blame him for his rage; if I had been through his experiences I'd be smashing things up too. There are trained volunteers helping people, but never enough.

I returned to Marcus "The Lion Heart" and his warm, "Hello brother," and a big grin cheered me up. We cracked on, finishing the last shelter in the dark. We left the cutting of the underlay (used to insulate walls, roof and floor) to the guys living there, and I give them my torch to keep and my knife and hammer to finish off the interior.

"Will you get that back do you reckon?" Marcus asks as we have a quick beer in the Sudanese bar.

"Probably..."

I've lent a few tools out and people are good at returning them, if you go back and ask...and they're in, apart from a staple gun that was lent to a massive guy to fix his tarpaulin. I asked him for it back and he just shook his head and said, "I keep." I wasn't going to argue, as he clearly wanted it more than me.

Marcus and I went out for food and drinks to a friendly pub in Calais. The volunteers are not welcome in most of the bars, as the locals do not appreciate the refugees. But the Family Pub always looks after us.

Later we tried another bar on the way home, just because, "Fuck em. Why not?" We received a much colder welcome. We kept calm, talked of peace and our experiences of the people we met there. We didn't raise our voices and we didn't find trouble. We had to calmly agree to disagree a few times, but had managed to evolve a few minds by the time we left. The highlight of ignorance was the Irish lads, who moved to Calais to open a wine warehouse - and had the nerve to complain about immigrants.

⌘

That night, I crashed with Marcus and had a shower and slept in a room for the first time that week. Nothing compared to some in The Jungle, but I definitely needed and appreciated it!

⌘

As adults, we all get to choose what we want to believe, how we want to behave. The effect of our actions is our responsibility, good and bad. We can help those who need it or we can ignore their desperate plight and make excuses based on fear, race, religion, money, time, or any number of reasons...but trust me, if you want to make a difference, you can.

Au Revoir Jungle

After chatting to various volunteers over breakfast at Marcus' hostel, I give as many as I can fit in a lift to the warehouse. I felt inspired by Ciaran a psychotherapist; he has seen the darkest side of The Jungle, yet radiates with positivity. I barely have the mental strength to build shelters in the mud without crying (something I could never do when they are being so strong). His work would break me.

We load the tools and charged drill batteries, and then with mixed feelings I head in for my last day in the Jungle. We had to wait for a few shelters to be dropped around the site, so found out where our shelters were going and were relieved to see flat ground. We returned to the road to wait for the van and I was pleased to see Amir outside the showers, "My friend," he says with a deep laugh as he crushes me in a bear hug.

The angry man with the wet tent from a few days ago comes out of his shelter and shakes my hand. Amir asks if I would like a free shower later (normally 2 Euros). I thank him and explain, with a sense of apology, that I must return home tomorrow, so will have a hotel tonight. He smiles and is very kind, pleased I will see my family soon and grateful for the small changes I have made while there.

Despite staying 2 days longer than planned, I feel guilty for leaving, I don't deserve to have a warm, safe home any more than any other human being and I have barely scratched the surface of the work needed to be done.

The neighbour of the angry man comes over to say hi. His name is Aru. I give him a ventilation plate to stop the condensation in his shelter. He was an interior designer in Iraq and has built a beautifully comfortable shelter and fitted it himself. He invites me for coffee. I'm not sure when the shelters will arrive so I tell Glen to call me when they're ready and I graciously accept his invite.

There are blankets ingeniously nailed to the walls with coke bottle lids to spread the weight, cushions to sit and lean on, a row of nails with clothes hanging and a small camping gas stove sits on a plinth with storage for cutlery and crockery. It's clean and organised and Aru beams with pride. He's done one hell of a job in an absolute hell-hole and he knows it. His friend Tahir joins us and we talk. Tahir was an electrician. He left after American bombs killed his parents and sister. He just wants to live in peace. If he had stayed, he would have been forced to fight for the Taliban and he doesn't believe in violence, so instead endured the only alternative.

Marcus knocks on the door. No van yet...he's immediately invited in. Marcus doesn't drink coffee, so is offered tea, which he gratefully accepts. The cigarettes are passed around next and we sit there, just four men, drinking a hot beverage, having a smoke and talking.

Aru tells us that he hasn't seen his family for 3 years. I take a moment to try to process the idea of not seeing my girls for nearly 3 years...it's impossible. Three years! I ask about his children: both girls, one is 5 the other is 2 and a half...it takes a moment for the maths to click; he has never met his youngest daughter! His pregnant wife and their daughter had the opportunity to get to safety in England, but it cost him a lot. He will go when he can, but it is much harder now. Marcus and I just look at each other - what can you say? He smiles a sad smile and says he hopes to get asylum, but only hopes. He doesn't risk getting on the trucks; he will be patient and just hope.

Glen pokes his head in and breaks the sadness with a cheery, "Yeah, it's Shelter-time!" Just what we all needed. We smile and hug, shake hands and wish each other the best as four men parting would - completely normal, but very different.

⌘

Marcus and I crack on with a shelter. It's for a teenager and his friends. There will be four of them sharing the space but he is the only one here. He doesn't speak English, but does what he can to help. The base goes down, sides go up, batons cut to length for the back wall and roof and a horizontal and vertical post to house the door. We're flying through it. As we start with the heavy plastic sheeting up for the walls, (which has come from a cut up marquee) a giant Sudanese guy appears. The kid we are helping is definitely not Sudanese.

He takes the staple gun we were using and using his massive build, pulls the heavy sheet tight and bangs in a few staples. This is most unusual. As a team of four we work our way round; the three of them pulling it tight and shooting staples to hold it in place, whilst I follow round putting clout nails in, to hold it permanently. My job takes longer but only takes one, so when the Sudanese chap offers food, Marcus does the right thing and accepts his hospitality. I'm not feeling well: light headed, sore throat and slightly feverish but it's barely midday so I crack on.

Last thing we put in is the tarpaulin roof. I unpack the tarpaulin with the young lad and I see his face drop. There were loads of holes in it. Rats, sun or just age had perished it and there was no way it would be waterproof. I reassured him that we would not use this and went in search.

None on the lorry, I went and found Mido: half German, half Syrian, a legend amongst the volunteers, she's been here for months, will be here for months more and can turn her hand to literally anything. I learn from Mido that we are out of heavy duty plastic, no more tarpaulins, or marquees until Monday.

I return to the dejected looking lad and explain the situation to Marcus on the way. Everything but a decent tarpaulin, and rain expected tonight. Nothing we could do now, we had more shelters to build. Maybe there would be spare plastic from that. I tried Amir at the showers with no luck, checked the distribution centre, and still no luck.

It was well after lunch and I was feeling really rough by now. Coughing and sweating from all the work, I hoped I just needed to eat. I promised I would return. He didn't look convinced, but thanked me and pressed two silver packets into my hand...Antibiotics. He pointed at my chest and looked concerned. He managed to communicate that he had a cough and these had made him better; he had two left. I took them with appreciation and dropped them to the medical point where they could be added and distributed as part of a full course and went to lunch.

I wasn't hungry and couldn't really eat. The others bullied me into forcing some lentils and a few chips down. Mido had a jar of golden liquid, it was a concoction of: lemon, honey, pepper, turmeric, and more. She poured some of the thick liquid into a cup and got some hot water. It burned, but felt good, numbing my throat, warming my insides and stopping the chills. "Keep your coat on even if you're hot." She said, in a motherly tone you wouldn't expect from a six foot, tattooed, blacksmith.

One of the volunteers was leaving and, as there were only a few shelters left to assemble, suggested I head back to the workshop with him and rest. I looked at the others and they all assured me they had it covered. I didn't want to leave the jungle like this, but felt maybe I had given it my all for now. I felt like a zombie.

I agreed and after a bit of jungle time, helping them get tools to the site and collecting my hammer from the shelter I'd lent it to the night before (they couldn't find my knife though), and finding Albert the renegade to give him the van keys, I was ready to collapse.

I trudged through the filth for the last time on my way to the car, the light already beginning to fade. I regretted not having achieved more that day. It was then I remembered there was still no roof on the earlier shelter and none to be found. I headed to the car, completely gutted, exhausted and felling helpless. I wanted to cry but never in The Jungle.

I got to the car. The driver wasn't there yet but wouldn't be long. Dave one of the volunteers sees me and comes to say hi. I tell him I feel like crap and he tells me to avoid mirrors. Charming. On the off chance I ask if he knows where I might get an emergency tarpaulin. Dave has two in his boot and gives me one.

With renewed energy, I force myself to run back into the jungle and to the shelter. I don't want to miss my lift, but this has to be done first. The lad is no longer there so I attempt to put it on myself. It wasn't long before someone who had been watching the midget struggle with the tarpaulin came over. It was his friend's roof and he would help me. We got it on and I nailed it tight in the corners. Having worked up a sweat, I was now freezing cold again and gave him hammer and nails and my last torch, and then I gave him my last knife and left him to put the last nails in the roof and insulate the shelter.

I ran back to the car. The driver was just arriving too - Jungle time - and so with regret I left the camp and took the first step on my journey back to my comfortable life.

⌘

I tried to sleep at the workshop with ear defenders on and waited for the others to return. It was 8pm by the time they did. Marcus jumped out of the van, "It was you wasn't it?", he yelled.

"What?" I replied.

Marcus smiled, "We all were just leaving the jungle when we realised that kid didn't have a roof. We went over to say sorry and there he was in his shelter, with a roof, very happy and warm." My face must have given it away. He gave me a massive hug and told me I was awesome. It was the best I'd felt for hours. Then he gave me my favourite knife back that the earlier guys couldn't find, but had kept looking for and returned to Marcus.

⌘

We headed to the hotel and after a hot shower and clean clothes, I felt almost human. We were all going home tomorrow, Tom, Cath and Glen, Albert and Marcus and I. As I sipped a few G&T's and they force fed me a few slices of pizza at the Family Pub, I listened to conversations of the people around me, the best you could ever hope to meet, everyone of them there to help others and everyone of us coming back to help again.

Return to The Jungle

Thank you for the donations:

I'd planned on taking the 4x4 over this time, but as I drove back from St Albans early on Saturday, before heading to play hockey, I realised that the Horse van may have to return with me... with it already full of clothes donations and fresh fruit and veg from Al Barka grocers, 200kg of potatoes, tinned food and loads more to come. The car wasn't going to cut it.

Fortunately knowing the good it would do, Christina didn't hesitate to say yes to a second loan of her vehicle. Having managed to partially dislocate my shoulder and fully dislocate my collar bone playing hockey: the loading was generally aided by various helpers and by Sunday morning the horse van was ready to roll. The clothes, tools, building materials, a table saw for the workshop and a trailer took up all the horse area, with the food donations going in the back. Stacked almost to the roof with various other food crammed in, on

and around were 600kg of sweet potatoes from Janey who grabbed a ride over with Marcus and I.

By the time we left the 3.5 ton van must have weighed about 5 tons and looked like it had been lowered! Marcus drove. I rested my arm in a sling and Janey shared with us the knowledge gained from her years of being an activist. We were enjoying each other's company so much that nobody noticed the fuel gauge until we cut out on the M20!

It started again, but after exiting the motorway, we cut out again at least 7 more times in the next 5 miles as we searched for fuel. Cruising down the hills, using the fuel that sloshed forward in the tank, turning her over and flying up the hills before the engine would cut out, we'd plead with the van to keep rolling to the brow as Marcus ekes out every last drop. Our excitement ended with a two-mile coast downhill that fortunately had a petrol station at its foot. We looked at each other incredulously; amazed we had made it so far on no fuel. The 'free-wheelers' laughed as we filled up and continued to Folkstone.

⌘

We arrived at the warehouse early and started by unloading the food: 25l bottles of vegetable oil from The Golden Elephant in Wheathampstead; potatoes from the Fish and chip shop; chick peas from Dildars; all the food from Al Barka and so much more. The reaction from the chefs and volunteers was amazing. There were yells of, "Sweet potatoes for days bruv."

"Fresh ginger is back in!"

Or just grabbing some oranges excitedly shaking them at me with glee and grinning,

"Yes! Vitamin C!"

You'd think they were the cold and hungry ones, they were so happy. It took a fair amount of time to unload the food, before moving on to the clothes, most of which had been sorted beautifully (the donations volunteers really appreciate this).

After clothes were out and two kids bikes were relieved by a lovely lady fixing bikes in the corner, she beamed as she gave them the once over and knew they didn't need any work and had spare inner tubes with them! Then it was round to the workshop to give them their stuff.

After donations and help had slowed over Christmas they were desperate for plastic sheeting, nails, screws, padlocks, tarpaulins, hinges...everything we'd bought really. Self build teams, who had been running low on everything, were more excited to see a hinge than any adult I've ever met.

The trailer would be handy for firewood transportation but Mido the workshop boss-lady had reservations about the table saw. With no blade guard and various skill levels in the workshop, it was put aside for potential use only by people with experience.

After unloading we went to the Brico to buy lengths of timber and clout nails (they didn't arrive from eBay in time) and then headed to The Jungle ready for building.

The move:

As you may be aware from the media, the French authorities had decided they wanted to clear a 100m perimeter around the camp near the road. This would allow them to protect their line and keep the refugees away from the lorries. Unfortunately this meant moving 1500+ people and their tents, shelters and belongings across a crowded wasteland. It was also an issue finding a new location for them. Space is in short supply, communities and groups are set up and politically it was a nightmare not just clearing and moving the people but finding a new place for them to go.

The atmosphere was very tense. In a few days the French would come and bulldoze everything. Moving that many people over that topography was clearly impossible. Unsurprisingly the refugees and their community leaders were angry, their human rights being ignored again.

We were caught in the middle, not knowing what to do. We wanted to get stuck in with the move, but we were there to support the people. Half the jungle wanted to protest, which would lead to violence from the police. If it came to this we'd stand shoulder to shoulder with our brothers and sisters.

Some residents wanted us to help them move because they didn't want trouble with the authorities, but we couldn't go against their community leaders and neither could they. In their eyes, we might as well join the CRS as disrespect their community's wishes.

That afternoon, while we waited to see what would happen, we built a new shelter in the safe zone for some teenage Afghan lads. They spoke excellent English and were into cricket, a couple of them having played semi professionally. They had dreams of playing County cricket in England.

There was a young boy nearby, threading a makeshift cricket ball through the tents, shelters and shit, back to a bowler who could have been his father. The boy was maybe 8 years old and the lads helping us build their shelter told us he had lost his mother and father to bombs before making the journey here and was now alone in The Jungle. The community looked after him now. There is a lot of this in the Jungle: shared responsibility, care for the community, sticking together to help protect the old, the young, and the vulnerable.

An old man asked me to help him move his shelter. I told him I couldn't today as the community leaders had decided to protest.

He said, "What leaders? I want to move. I don't want trouble," and left, shaking his head and wringing his hands. There was an atmosphere of tension, fear and uncertainty. The jungle was on a knife-edge and you could feel it building as the impossible situation kept rearing its head.

⌘

As ever the jungle conditions weren't allowed to dampen spirits or hospitality. Sweet, milky tea was frequent and a hot meal provided.

We built the shelter as a team. The Afghan lads worked hard. They were going to be sleeping there and were pleased to see us giving it as much care and attention as they were, to ensure it would be warm and dry. We laughed and joked, like guys on building sites do. It doesn't matter what language you speak. If I'm behind a roll of insulation, holding it whist it's being nailed by one of the Afghans to a wall, and yell, "Ow!" before laughing at their worried gasp, trust me it's funny in any language.

It was dark by the time we finished and gave them their padlock, at maybe 8.30pm. The usual hugs and thanks were given, we wished them the best and told them I hoped to see the young lad playing cricket for England one day. They said they would keep playing cricket with him and look after him until he was allowed into the UK - there is always hope, I suppose.

Uncertainty:

Returning to the Jungle a second time was different; not just knowing what to expect, but also the reception. A large white van with horses on it is apparently quite distinctive. I was greeted with smiles, waves and even a few cheers as the residents showed their appreciation for our return to help.

From my work alongside them, I have learnt that many would thank Allah for our presence, believing it's not our choice but that we have been chosen and sent to them. I don't think I believe in a God, but I couldn't possibly be arrogant enough to discount this. I feel like I have been awakened, maybe there are forces I am unaware of that move me to action, but I'm still sceptical.

⌘

But I'm just here to help and my reasons are simple, I'm needed and I can.

⌘

Jungle friends come to the window as I thread my way through the people at walking pace and tell me their shelters are warm and I am a good man for coming back. The selfish warm glow of doing good comes back and I feel a little guilty. This time, instead of pushing it away, I embrace it and decide that it's OK to feel good and that I should use it as fuel for the work ahead. Maybe there are no unselfish acts, but they might as well be positive ones.

I keep inching along the muddy road, taking care not to splash mud from puddles on what might be someone's only clean trousers. Nasser finds me, grinning like a Cheshire Cat, we hug through the window. I agree to help him move his shelter, but we still have to wait for the go ahead from the community leaders. I tell him there are many meetings today, but to have their documents ready, in case the bulldozers come, and to pack their belongings ready to go. When it all starts, its will be crazy. He tells me they will be ready and Marcus and I keep going along the road to the build site.

We were building six emergency shelters for women and children, behind the church. With teams of two and three, there were around fifteen of us. While they unloaded the van, I kept an eye on the tools and pointed with my good arm to where the various materials needed to go to keep this build organised. There's a lot to do. If the people don't move in the next few days and the bulldozers clear the tents, after more terror, tear-gas and violence these people will need somewhere to go.

It's about midday by the time we start to build. The morning organiser meetings, uncertainty as to what we were allowed to do, loading/unloading the van and getting to the site, meant we would only get these emergency shelters up before dark and nobody was allowed to move from their current stand until their 'elected leaders' say so.

6 shelters only house 24-30 people and there were 1500 to move. There might be a few more teams in The Jungle building, but this task was impossible. Low materials had meant there hadn't been enough parts of shelters or transport to build many more. But the materials we brought were being turned into shelter components and more would be here soon, but how soon?

It's impossible to feel low for long with Marcus around, with his can-do attitude. He also smiles all the time; a proper smile that sets you at ease despite his size. Volunteers, refugees, hard men, women and especially children, all warm to Marcus, touching his long dreads and calling him Rastaman. Soon we're levelling and screwing together pallets as floors and joining the frames.

Unlike previous builds, there weren't any residents helping hammer the plastic on with clout nails, bringing tea or taking pride in their work, or thanking us. It was full steam ahead and with a combination of painkillers, I felt little pain as we worked efficiently. We had a week in the jungle under our belts, a good team and the sense of being only at the beginning of a mammoth task driving us all forward.

It was dark by the time we all finished. Our shelter went up reasonably quickly, with Marcus taking the high bits and me working at my optimal level, using my left arm for holding screws and nails and my right for everything else. Once a shelter was finished the volunteers would help get another finished off, so we could all tidy up and go home in the various shared transport.

When Marcus and I were done there was the usual quick job here and there: collecting tools you lent and said you would return for;

the promises of a one minute, quick fix, that due to Jungle time turns into a five minute trudge through the mud, a ten minute wrestle with conditions and equipment, a slog back picking your way through guy lines, shelters and makeshift fences that turn into dead ends. But we do it, never complaining when someone you're waiting for apologises and says, "Jungle time". We understand it's hard to say no, when it's a simple job.

We all do it to ensure other humans sleep safe or dry tonight. A fixed lock, a tarpaulin to waterproof the roof, there are a lot of one minutes in the jungle and the result is a black hole for time that leaves one bewildered as to how it got so late again.

⌘

Marcus and I returned to our hotel for a shower and headed to the Family Pub for a late dinner and chat to the other volunteers and the staff, while we await developments. Important decisions made by the Jungle elders are always made at night.

Next morning we get to the workshop and tool up for the day: hammers, crow bars...but not for violence.

⌘

There's a buzz around, as the word is out. The community leaders have resolved to find the most peaceful solutions. They will peacefully protest against the infraction on their human rights, but for the safety of their communities, they will move. They are not happy about it and I don't blame them.

They are human beings, forced by other people's bullshit wars from good jobs. Now living in a muddy shit-hole, built on a refuse dump full of rats, disease and asbestos. To add to that, they are now being herded like livestock and forced into living quarters that would make a battery hen feel claustrophobic. All to ensure that they cannot escape the hell they are trapped in, to stop their political protests of slowing traffic to force industry and media to ignore them no longer, to make them easier targets for rubber bullets and tear-gas.

We hear the perimeter has grown but the deadline may be extended, if we do well today. So everybody heads to The Jungle ready to dismantle and rebuild shelters for the total insanity that will be Jungle Moving.

Moving:

We spend the next few days in a similar pattern: early mornings unscrewing shelters from their pallet bases, allowing the residents to carry them to a new location, while we unscrewed more shelters. We would then build self-builds when they arrived on site and then later in the day we would reassemble shelters that had been moved inside the perimeter.

There was a lovely bunch of Iraqi lads who had taken the initiative and found a site to move to, physically torn their shelters apart and moved them to the other side of the jungle with all their belongings on the first morning they were told OK. They needed help screwing it all together and needed some new plastic for the roof etc. So we got stuck in. Before we knew it, we were helping lead about ten groups of refugees rebuild their shelters, some guys translating for the other ones, lending out tools to anyone who needed one, but always with a look in the eye and a circular motion of the finger indicating, "This comes back to me". They almost always did. I lent out as many tools as I had: handfuls of nails, saws, staple guns, screws and drills until all the shelters around us were waterproof and warm and all our batteries were dead, leaving hammers and nails for them to finish off. Hammers and nails are always handy and get passed around; so one hammer in the jungle is worth ten in my hand.

There was a moment when I had to take a saw back from an Afghan lad, who wanted to cut a long branch, which his Sudanese neighbour was using as a border fence. Explaining to him like a jungle bound Robert Frost in Mending Wall, that, "Good fences make good neighbours," and more importantly, fence or not, it's not your wood.

The Sudanese guy was very friendly and appreciated it. Boundaries need to be set and relationships here are built on mutual respect. We would help where we could, when we could, but generally tried to make best use of our skills. There were bodies for teamwork. The rally call had been sent, heard and answered from the UK and elsewhere. The Jungle was alive; it was as though all the volunteers from the past had arrived en mass to perform an anarchist miracle, working with the refugees to save as many shelters as we could. The area to be cleared was emptying slowly.

One morning, after taking apart a dozen shelters that were ready to go Marcus and I were asked to lend a hand lifting an entire shelter onto a flat bed. As the twenty or so volunteers and residents heaved it upwards, a rat the size of a small dog ran straight across my feet, probably disappointed his warm home and food supply was moving. The lady next to me screamed (I swear it was her) as more rats fled the nest and we all staggered to the trailer with the floating house.

I get a call from Tom, a lovely guy on the build team; along with Pete, Jack and many others, he keeps everything moving and deals with the build crews, the workshop, driving the vans, the residents who all want shelters and the bureaucrats. Today we are building for the Kurds.

As we unload, a fourteen year old boy with poor English tells me he is in a tent in the mud, with other boys. Unable to help with heavy lifting, I go and have a look. It's him and another three boys aged fourteen, fifteen and seventeen, in a tent in the cold. I tell him I'll sort it and he looks sceptical. I take him back to Tom, who agrees to get me a shelter in the next run; we will have to help them build it of course. I tell the boy I will be back at around 4pm to build him a shelter. Lost in translation a little, he says "Tomorrow?"

"Today...later, today." I reply. I think he understands.

Another lad with excellent English and bright blue eyes comes over. He is in the same position and asks for a shelter. There are components left for one in the van, ready for a build team, but all the build teams are on shelters so he will have to wait. I recognise him from my last trip when he spoke to me and his name went on the list.

"Can you build it, if we give it to you?" I ask. He looks unsure. "If I give you saw, hammer and nails, can you build it?" I ask again.

"Yes, he says. I have no tools, but we can build."

We unload the van and his friends ferry the materials to their new site.

As I grab my tools from the horse van, ready to head off to the Kurds to build. Blue eyes grabs me and hugs me, grinning as he runs off to do the first real 'self-build' I'd seen.

The young lads look at me again and say,

"Today?"

"Today." I reassure them.

Kurdish resistance:

We had 3 shelters to build in the Kurdish area, which is just inside the perimeter. Overlooked by the road now, in the distance across empty scrub, there's a mixture of clad pre-fabs, caravans for families and the usual tents and self-builds but the ground is reasonable and it should be a good build.

Whenever it's time to unload, my arm starts to ache and the sling I occasionally rest it in comes out. I prep the mud foundations, picking up rocks, old socks and nappies with my gloved right hand and kicking the ground level as best I can. Materials are ferried to the site from the van and I point to where I want the three sets of components to go for an efficient build: each teams door, roof, walls and eleven lengths of timber etc. in order of use, as close to them as possible, while being out of everyone's way.

We start to build around midday and the bases start to go down. We have about eight people working. A lovely girl called Emma takes the one next door with a couple of others and I crack on with Marcus.

The children from the caravan are bored and a four year old boy insists on helping me do the first twenty screws. Using an electric screwdriver is probably the most fun he's had for a while, so I take my time and we build a floor together and jump on it to make sure it's solid. He goes and joins his friends, who come back as we start to build the framework of the walls and roof. They get bored again and when we don't let them help, as it's not safe for so many and time is a factor, they sulk and throw dirt on the floor.

The Rastaman roars with a smile and chases them away as they scatter, laughing. One of the mothers scolds them and smiles at us. We smile back and that is enough.

We get the framework nearly done when Marcus is asked to fix a caravan window. He looks at me and says, "One minute?" The window is within eye-shot and all the high work is done so I tell him to crack on. Other shelters were further ahead, with some of the plastic walls on already. We are doing well.

Timber is done and I've tidied up and I'm just having a smoke break with Emma. I'm ready to start the plastic and am just waiting on Marcus to finish up when I spot twenty five Kurdish men with hammers and sticks heading in our direction. I look at Marcus up a ladder and let him know we might have trouble.

But Marcus wasn't close enough to intercept them with "the smile" and they were heading straight for me.

I moved towards them, away from Emma and attempted a smile. I'm not sure if my standing around pointing during the unloading process had me labelled as the boss, but right now they were surrounding me and they were not happy. Two of them had good English, one spoke almost as fluently as you or I. I don't speak any Kurdish, yet.

"We want you to stop building and leave," he said. "Right now, I want you to stop building, take your tools and leave."

I introduced myself and he gave me his name. We'll call him Jon.

"Can we please finish first, so we can build more?" I asked.

"No, stop now and leave," he replied decisively. "You do not build enough for us, you build for everyone else who makes trouble and we are very angry. Stop work now."

This wasn't my call. I had no authority to stop a build in a humanitarian crisis. We could be putting a roof over people's heads tonight. But this was for the Kurds and they were telling us to stop. So I made a decision and shouted for everyone to stop building and come out of the shelters. Unlike in my own home, strangely everyone listened and came out of the shelters; maybe the sling had fooled them too.

The Kurds issue, which was delivered aggressively, was that we were only building three shelters for them. In their view the Afghans make more trouble and get more shelters. The leader looked me dead in the eye and said, "We Kurds are a peaceful people but we can make trouble if our people need it."

I believed him.

I tried to explain that the people here didn't choose where to build and we're building as many as we could for as many as possible. He said he understood and to get the Chief down here.

I phoned Tom, who spoke to Nico, who would be fifteen minutes as she was on the other side of The Jungle. I agreed we would tidy our tools and prepare to leave while Nico was called, but we would do no more work. I sorted and stacked my toolboxes as everyone tidied up. I placed the insulation rolls inside the shelter frame, put the plastic cladding and roof over that in case it rained and left a hammer, Stanley Knife and nails in the centre of the floor. It was everything someone needed to finish the build.

A young volunteer asked about keeping a hammer handy, just in case the Kurds had some weapons of sorts. I couldn't blame him; it had crossed my mind for a moment. I told him I didn't want to see a single tool in hand and to do whatever the Kurds wanted. We were leaving, so there shouldn't be a problem.

I sat on my toolboxes and had another smoke with Emma. She was shaken by the whole experience and I gave her a hug. Nico still hadn't arrived, but as we smoked the Kurds were returning with greater numbers.

It didn't look great and I asked Emma if she wanted to go. She did and I told her to leave. I went to talk to Jon. Emma didn't leave, but stayed along with the other volunteer, all unsure of what was going to happen next. Marcus stood next to me and we went to meet Jon.

Jon said they wanted to build with us. After they had scared the shit out of the volunteers, I wasn't keen on agreeing to that and I pointed at the shelter and said, "No, you have everything you need to finish and plenty of people with plenty of hammers. You have scared people who are here to help you and there are others who need our help."

Jon looked at me and with a hint of apology in his voice said, "No, please Ben, we will build together." I understood he was in a difficult position, trying to manage and take care of his people with a hundred opinions and this was a reasonable compromise.

I checked for a few nods from the volunteers and Emma and announced loudly, "Together we will build."

The other two shelters were appointed Kurdish helpers and we got back to work. With the extra hands we got going and even managed to free up people for another build. In my shelter there were two builders with me and we smashed it. We quickly made friends and while alone they apologised for the trouble. I sympathised and together we built the most beautifully insulated shelter I'd made.

Nico had since told me to give the padlocks to Jon, once the shelters were done. It was dark by the time we had all finished. I'd locked the shelters and explained to the people that I couldn't give them the keys to the shelters they have just helped build, then found Jon and ensured that the keys were going to the people who built them.

Marcus came and gave me one of his bear hugs and told me I'd done great. We hadn't eaten and it was about 7pm.

Three hours late, I went to find the young fourteen year old from that morning and told him I would be back in one hour and I would build him a shelter tonight. He didn't look so sure.

We went to the Afghan flag for some Chicken, rice and beans with sweet tea and friendly owners; it's always lively and warm. We got chatting to a friendly Palestinian character with excellent English who played a game with raisins, which he strangely always won. When we ordered food he jumped up and said, "I am cooking for these gentlemen!" And bustles into the kitchen. The staff, clearly familiar with our new friend, happily obliged and I guessed it wasn't his first time in their kitchen.

We started chatting to a nice guy from North Africa who was trying to set up a Barbers in the jungle and all laughed at our friend Kit's stories. He had been strimming the bushes with a heavy-duty bit of machinery and had hit loads of nappies, poo and worst - a carton of sour milk. He did have a face mask but had accidentally put it down in poo at some point, and then taken twenty minutes to work out why everywhere smelled of poo!! Sometimes my job seems easy.

We ate our meal, famished and in need of energy. A group of Afghan lads came in whilst Marcus and I waited for Tom to return from a Jungle meeting. We chatted to them. They were in their teens, had learnt English from the movies and were happy to practise. They joked about how many people we could get in the horse van and I said I'd go by boat if I were them.

"Do you have a boat?", they asked.

"Not yet," I winked.

They were all skilled or educated, all wanting to come to work. Not one wanted handouts, just a chance, an opportunity to be human, to live, to work, to be safe. We had a smoke together and more tea. We were warm and comfortable. The people were friendly, I was tired and I wanted to stay. We said goodbye, paid and thanked our hosts and left.

⌘

It was cold outside and the idea of building another shelter wasn't inviting, but I had promised, and Tom and Marcus weren't going to let me do it on my own.

We arrived at the boys to find them huddled in their tent. They couldn't believe it when I poked my head in and said, "We build shelter now."

"Now?" They were still unsure.

"Now, tonight! Now, now," I answered.

Marcus roused them and soon we were ferrying materials. My shoulder didn't hurt; it was too late in the day for pointing. As we moved the materials in there was a group of about 6 men. I had seen them throughout the day dismantle and move a huge board clad, solid roof shelter on their own. They were more tired than us, but still going.

As I passed, I said hello and asked if they needed anything. Someone with good English asked for a drill to put in the screws that hold it together. I said we were using ours but could give them a hand in a bit. I then decided we had enough hands and drills so I went and worked with them, while Tom, Marcus and the boys carried on building the shelter I'd promised them.

These guys were from Iraq and were great, hoisting me up into the roof to screw the metal cladding on, putting the screws in the holes ready for me to screw in. We worked fast and with few words. After the roof and walls and being on various men's shoulders, I put security screws in the hinges and latches and even made them a handle for the door. Funnily enough it was the only carving I did on site. There were exhausted hugs and words of thanks and praise before I returned to help the others finish the shelter.

We finished at around 11.30pm, glad to see the boys safe and warm, in an OSB sheet clad shelter, with a lock and insulation. Barely older than my ten year old daughter and living in fear and squalor, they were some of the happiest faces I saw in the jungle when they locked their shelter and said good night.

⌘

It had been a good days work and we were completely exhausted...so obviously we went to the Family Pub for a well-earned drink.

Another busy day:

Marcus and I allowed ourselves a rare lie-in and wandered down for breakfast about 9am. When the phone rang, I was tucking into a fried egg. The yoke perfectly cooked and ready to burst all over my French bacon and toast. It was Tom. He had had a phone call. The Kurds would like us to build again with them but only if I ran the build. Having built a trust and our team having worked effectively alongside the Kurdish community, it was nice to know everyone's efforts were appreciated.

Worryingly, I had been asked for by name by the Kurdish leaders. I had come here to follow, to build where told, to be one of the many volunteers and do what I could to help. But this was potentially an olive branch. Although I couldn't make a long term commitment to the project like others, (Tom, Mido, Pete, Jack and so many more, whose relentless efforts motivated me to do what I could) right now, what I could do, is build relationships and shelters with the Kurds, so of course I said yes.

⌘

Needless to say, breakfast was quickly polished off with a quick update for Marcus.

⌘

We headed to the workshop to grab supplies. Along with the materials, fixings and tools for the three self-builds we would be working with, I grabbed a load of extra tools. The answer to the rally call had brought 100 hammers, saws and loads of materials. Whilst they wouldn't last forever, they were needed in the jungle in this crisis, so I checked with the boss and loaded up saws, hammers, random nails that were no use for self builds and a few more bits and pieces.

⌘

Before we knew it, we were in the horse van and heading to the jungle again.

⌘

My first stop was the showers. After the usual hug and kiss on the cheek from my friend and a quick exchange of, "How did you sleep?" and the big move, I switched a couple of dead drill batteries for a couple of charged ones and were sent on our way with blessings for the day ahead. We met Tom and headed to see the build site.

We met 'Jon', head of the Kurdish family. The locations and allocations had been decided by the elders. Against fire regulations, one of the shelters was not facing North in the direction of evacuation. Something we had been firmly schooled on by our elders the day before. Jon seemed pretty set on the layout and it was their dwelling so I decided to let that bureaucratic bullshit slide and build it where they wanted.

Whilst the unloading was going on, I went around the tight-knit community and said, "Toni, (Hi) " to the various people around. The children were already fed and running around.

A man in a tent asked me if I had any plastic for his roof so we went to the nearby van. The tarpaulin didn't have any eyelets in it so I showed him the trick of wrapping a stone in the edge of the tarpaulin and then tying string around them to give it an anchor point. A family man from a large clad shelter opposite him translated before translating for a few more people. I gave out a role of duct tape, a couple of hammers, nails, a few saws, tarpaulins and timber.

The family man asked me where to return the tools and I told him to hold onto them and let the community use them. I promised to return with more tomorrow and headed to the community build behind, already noisy with the bangs of hammers and the sound of saws. It was music to my ears.

The build went well. There were no political protests; it was all hands on deck.

We had six guys helping us; the two guys with me were tradesmen, an electrician and a plumber, they were skilled and accurate and we had a good laugh. Whilst their English was broken, we managed to communicate as ever. They'd often criticise each other's work and point at how I was doing it and scolding each other. I'd smile and say, "No problem. It's good," and another exchange without need for translation would take place.

When it comes to the insulation, it looks awful when you start. We were using the silver bubble wrap but whichever insulation, no matter how tight you pull it, when you nail it in the various available beams around the edge it always sags with huge air gaps. I got the usual look and question, "Problem?"

"No problem. It's time for the Magic!" I say, with a confident grin and pull a couple of staplers out of my toolbox.

I staple along the face of all the rafters as one of my friend follows suit and the other hammers nails in the vital points. We then staple again along the inside and outside of the rafters, securing it on all sides, wrapping the insulation tight around the wood and taking up the slack. I hand over the other stapler and check on the other builds, before heading to the showers for fresh batteries.

One battery is charged; the other is dead. His generator had stopped working. One of the guys who stayed there has put the wrong oil in and it's seized. A mechanic friend is coming but he needs an adjustable spanner. I have one in my toolbox on site.

By the time I get back to the shelter, it looks like a space ship. The lack of windows means a wind-up lamp is usually the only light source so reflective materials are great and warm.

I give them the thumbs up: "It's done!"

They grin and we have a quick hug and handshake, a good job done.

"Best shelter yet," I say, not for the first or last time. They have a smoke whilst I quickly run to and from the showers to drop off the spanner.

Once again I had to lock the shelters

we had built together and take the keys to Jon. In the Jungle nothing is certain; the guys I'd worked with, a man and his wife who had worked with Emma and a couple more lads who were with Marcus, were all despondent. Whilst Marcus used the time to be general fix-it man, I found Jon and gave him the keys.

Jon then gave the Kurdish shelter builders their keys and everyone was happy. They thanked me and hugged me and went to fetch their belongings.

Jon thanked me for all my help. I told him it was my pleasure and we hugged. When we were alone he apologised to me for the trouble. I said it was OK and that I understood, he was doing what he had to for his community and it had been successful. He smiled knowingly and said. "Yes, not the way I wanted, but we have some more shelters now." He carried on to the next job of his day and I continued to mine.

⌘

Next build was three more shelters; this time on the other side of camp. We threaded the van past the melee of volunteers, residents, trailers and floating houses with legs and cries of,

"Left. Right. Up. Stop." It's a difficult task navigating the jungle with a team of twenty people and a dozen languages.

When we arrived near the dome, now a hive of construction as everyone got stuck into rebuilding what they had salvaged, we found we had a new build team. Ben, Tom, Tom, Ben, Tom and James. We tried swapping James but there were no more Ben's available and he's pretty handy so we let him stay. Phil, from the kitchen, was also with us having a change of scenery. He is a young, intelligent lad who just gets on with it.

We levelled the ground and built two of the shelters facing each other with an extended roof that met, to offer a dry area outside for boots and hanging wet clothes. The teenage Afghans took the opportunity to do something proactive for a change, bored of months of waiting for their dreams of asylum to come true. We built fast and lent out tools and gave away any materials we had left in the van. It was already getting dark again and cold. I had some spare silver bubble insulation in the van and when a young lad told us he had moved his whole shelter but his insulation had been stolen, I gave him the lot plus a staple gun and a load of staples.

All were returned with thanks, including a couple of left over rolls he asked if I could give to his neighbour. I met the neighbour; he had a hammer so I gave him extra nails and he got to work immediately.

Another warm shelter sorted, I picked my way back to the nearly finished shelters. The sound of work rang everywhere, the light from head torches illuminating all the shelters, workers and smiling, tired faces. The sense of unity giving the jungle a new positive feel of hope and survival.

⌘

We left many hammers, saws and pots of nails in various hands in various communities that day. Staplers always come back due to their finite use, but they will happily work through a mixed box of nails more efficiently than the workshop apprentice.

If we give them the tools and materials they will build for themselves. They are not helpless. Some need our help. They are cold and hungry and I couldn't perform surgery any more than a surgeon can build a shelter. But there are many skilled and innovative people in The Jungle and we should aim to help them, help themselves.

The residents gathered and about forty people all waving and smiling guided us, in a seven-point turn. It was properly dark by the time we headed off from the dome past the black market, where socks and gloves are sold on the road. It's always the hardest time and place to navigate in a large vehicle and at night the residents in mob mode are slow to move and have more of a, "Fuck off do-gooder. We've finished for the day. It's social time attitude." But today there is positivity and as we creep past, taking care not to splash mud, there are more smiles and much singing.

We have someone in the back with the tools but nobody tries the door. I have the window right down and lean out smiling and saying hello or good night to anyone who makes eye contact. People are friendly and start to move and even usher others out of the way and wave us through with a few cheers.

We stop at the shower and grab the charged batteries. The generator is purring away and the guys are around the wood burner chatting. They all look up and smile, waving me over. Sometimes I find time for a chat, but it's late, I'm getting tired now and there's still more to do. My friend tries to give me the spanner back, but I tell him to hold on to it just in case. We say good night and I head back out through the blanket curtain and door into the cold.

We find Pete and Jack on the final build: a clad prefab behind the Sudanese church. They have a few helpers and it's going well. I set my toolboxes down and ask how I can help. Pete grins and tells me he heard about my heroics yesterday. I assume he means the Kurds, laugh it off and tell him I heard about his (a post pub encounter of another nature).

The guys exchange glances and tell us they have it covered and we can head off for a shower and dinner! I want to kiss them! I hadn't realised how exhausted I was. The adrenalin, the collective energy and the strong painkillers were wearing off and I was totally knackered. I put the tools in the van and waited for one-minute-Marcus to return from a mission of repair.

As we left The Jungle there was a feeling of celebration around, a unity. I finally realised that maybe we had done it. The perimeter was almost completely empty. Maybe the impossible had been made possible, with all the people answering the call for help in that emergency, all the long and short-term volunteers and the residents working together, differences and disputes set aside, as everyone found a common enemy in the authorities and a common goal in succeeding to move 1500 people to safety and collectively give those authorities a big, "Fuck you!"

Maybe we had won and proved that together we can achieve anything and the weak can beat the strong when they are one. I'll be honest, tired as I was, that felt pretty damn good.

We headed for a shower and on to the Pub for dinner. The place is rammed with the hundred plus volunteers pouring out onto the street. The mood is jubilant, everyone smiling and cheerful, even the gloomy ones. Many are still in their muddy boots and clothes from a weekend of hard work and we have to battle our way to the door.

We're told by the overworked waitress that clearly they are full: no tables, no food, we can order beer and she will bring it outside. We agree to the beer option and Marcus goes in to set up a tab.

A moment later, Zazu, the bar manager, is tapping me on the shoulder. We say hello and kiss each other on the cheek and he drags me inside. "For Marcus and you we can find a table." he beams, as I see a table of four paying and leaving hurriedly.

I feel guilty and look at the floor as they slide past muttering in French. For about two seconds I feel bad and then I sit down next to Marcus and Zazu and some beers arrive and we talk and drink. Baptiste the waiter has come in on his night off and joins us for a while too before Zazu had to work and Baptiste chases some skirt and Phil and a few volunteers join us for dinner. We eat and then give up our table, drinking and circulating, swapping stories and enjoying the moment of collective achievement against the odds.

That night I collapsed into bed and despite my shoulder fell asleep immediately: The job done, the mind done, and the body done.

Bon-voyage

When Marcus and I had planned to return to Calais there hadn't been an emergency move expected. By the time to leave had come there was too much left to be done to go. We knew we really could make a difference and didn't have any engagement more important than the task at hand. With the immediate blessing of my wife, who understood the task at hand, and the encouraged blessing of my daughter, we had stayed two days extra but today we were leaving.

Exhausted from a busy week, we had a lie-in. No phone calls. No emergency. Rest. We skipped breakfast and headed to the workshop. Yesterday's seed of a plan had formed. We went to the workshop, saying our goodbyes to various volunteers as we went.

Then, with Mido's blessing, we collected all the donated tools and fixings that nobody would use. I grabbed a load of boxes and buckets and started to fill. Any saw with a sharp edge that was tatty looking, a bit rusty or old with a wooden handle went into the box. People in the workshop or doing self builds would always grab a shiny one, so of the hundred saws that were not out doing self builds or being utilised in the workshop, there are dozens of saws that hadn't been touched for months. There were thirty pairs of pliers in a box. The workshop might need a few pairs, so I took twenty five. In another box full of spanners, if there were more than three of the same size they went in the bucket. There were fifty Screwdrivers and forty hammers, most of which had wooden handles so had a layer of dust. All these "crappy bits and bobs" added up to a full floor in the back of the van. It also offered some clear space in the workshop, allowing Mido to organise it even closer toward perfect order, amid perfect chaos.

Any pots, boxes, buckets or tins of mixed nails or screws were split into groups. We grabbed any obsolete plastic, fixings, hand tools, duct tape and more and we headed off.

Our first stop was the Afghan Flag restaurant. I had a massive bag of DVDs that were unsuitable for the children's area, but ideal for the young lads who were made welcome and warm there. They thanked me and one guy took five from the bag. I smiled and gave him the whole lot, pointing at the young lads already hanging out.

"For the boys," I said and he smiled and shook my hand, calling to the boys, who came over said thank you and started deciding what to watch.

We headed to the Kurdish area next and said goodbye to the people there. Leaving a load more saws, hammers and nails with the family man with good English.

Having previously heard the Kurds complaints about being unfairly treated with shelter allocation. Marcus and I then visited the communities in all corners of The Jungle. We dropped tools and fixings with the Sudanese and Eritreans, the Iraqis and Iranians, Afghans and Kurds.

I said goodbye to my friend at the showers and gave him a head torch and a load of batteries, hopefully nobody would mix up the oil with the diesel when the generator runs out at night again. I left him my spanner too and a promise to return again soon.

I thanked him for the charging and he just shrugged.

"It's for the people," he smiled.

Thanking me for my hard work and late nights, and all the volunteers for what had been achieved, he gave me one of his 6'6" bear hugs, kissed me firmly on both cheeks and called me his special brother. With 8 languages under his belt he was in tune with a lot of groups in The Jungle and saw the big picture.

We visited a carpenter I'd given timber to near the dome, his shelter looking impressive and safe. He had been helping various teenagers the day before so I knew he was a good guy. All tools were given not lent, with the instructions that the tools were entrusted to that person to be used and returned by all in the community regardless of nationality.

What can I say? I'm an optimist.

Once the van was spent of it's ironmongery bounty, we finally visited Nasser and the guys for tea. Well I did. Marcus had a one-minute repair to attend to.

I tried to sneak into a shop and buy some biscuits but Nasser spotted me and insisted on paying and we headed to his shelter.

Between the twelve of them, they had moved everything they owned in the world to the opposite side of The Jungle. I had seen them all at various times helping, carry buildings or loading and unloading pallets for people. They had worked tirelessly as a team and to help others and they had done a great job.

They still had one shelter to assemble but were waiting until tomorrow for plastic. They understood it all takes time and had squeezed six to a shelter the night before.

Today, whilst they waited, they were building their community kitchen and Nasser apologised profusely, "No coffee today Benedict's. The kitchen is under construction." He chose his words beautifully and checked they were right with me.

"Under construction, perfect English," I encouraged and he beamed. He has always called me Benedict's, since I gave him a business card that said, Benedict's Fine Furniture, so we could arrange fixing his roof months ago. I have never corrected him and like it when I hear a happy call of "Benedict's" across The Jungle and know it's him.

⌘

All twelve, a mixture of Afghans, Iranians and Pakistanis (you can see why I like this bunch) downed tools and joined us for tea and biscuits whilst we discussed the crazy past week and their on-going wait.

I have no answers as to when our government might wake up to their situation. I can only offer hope and tell them that I feel the balance is tipping and the more empathetic humans of our country are on their side. We drink lots of sweet milky tea and wait for Marcus. The 1-minute job has taken 45mins as they usually do. Marcus apologises and we both say, "Jungle time," and smile. The guys understand and laugh.

Mohammed has been keeping an eye on the time, tells me it's getting late and we don't want to miss our crossing. Marcus downs a tea that he is slowly beginning to enjoy more than endure and we say our goodbyes. They have everything they need to finish building, but their plastic is flapping so I tell Nasser to come with me to the van.

I give him my staple gun. It's brilliant, I've held onto it all week because a lot have been abused and every person I lent it to brought it back, post 'dad lecture'. I give it to Nasser with a two litre bottle of staples and tell him to look after it and help others to finish their shelters when his were done. We hugged and I promised to return soon. I asked if he needed anything and he replied," Only you and England brother," and we hugged again.

⌘

We drove out of The Jungle, past the rebuilding shelters and the busy people, hammers, saws and drills ringing out as residents worked and sang. It was a completely different place to the panicked and tense Jungle we had experienced a few days ago. The unachievable now achieved, the people working 'united'. Marcus and I had a hug and patted each other in the backs.

As we left, I saw a young girl with a smile on her face, ride past on a bicycle, a friend had donated it and I had brought it over with my daughters.

As we drove on I met Rosie and her parents. Rosie is the Jungle baby, born into this hell. Her parents, despite their situation, were glowing with love and pride. They gratefully received the packs of baby wipes I had in the van door, ready for just the right person and a spare padlock and keys, just in case.

⌘

An empty van, broken bodies but emblazoned spirits. Whilst the residents and long-term volunteers worked on, we headed home. Exhausted and amazed at their resilience. Our job was done, for now.

Back to the jungle:

I couldn't believe my eyes when I saw the new perimeter around The Jungle. Having helped move the communities clear previously, I knew the scale to be expected. But I still wasn't prepared. The tents and shelters were gone, the rubbish and filth and undulating ground all removed. Along the whole length of the motorway, with its double fences and patrolling thugs, the machines had scraped back the rough ground to flat greyish, brown mud, which now formed an earthen moat around the camp. The excess soil and shit pushed up in a wall surrounding the jungle in a high barrier, leaving the ground between as barren and clear as any prison camp.

It was still early in the jungle as I crossed no-man's-land, the CRS officers noting the number plate and showing no emotion as I smiled and nodded as friendly as I would be to any other human, I like to think it fucks with them a bit too.

The few early risers in the Jungle are going about their mornings: washing, using the toilets, fetching the water or breakfast. Morning people seem happy, nodding and smiling as I crept past. I guess if you're grumpy in the morning you might as well stay in bed here.

I rubbed my eyes, trying to wake up and take it in. It had been a long night.

The 4x4, loaded to the roof with donations made it fifty miles from Dover before it died. I was with Tom. He runs the self builds and had returned for a few days off. We pulled on our jackets and exited the vehicle. We climbed the embankment whilst we waited for the AA, entertaining ourselves by watching three lads chopping up a stolen vehicle in the woods above the M20.

After returning home on a flat bed, unloading, loading the once more sequestered horse van and heading off into the night, it was already becoming a long day. By the time we arrived at Dover, had been diverted to Dunkirk and then driven on to Calais, it was 4.30am as we crawled into the pine and OSB sheet shelter next to the workshop.

I dragged my body out of bed and was unloading the van by 9am, coffee in hand: clout nails, padlocks and other bits for the workshop, a table football table, dart board, punch bag and gloves for the boys shelter (under construction), as well as various clothes and other collections. The self-builds would be an hour yet, so I had headed in alone.

First stop was the dome, a central hub of positivity and community spirit. It has letters and photos from residents and holds cultural and social events and activities. This was the first time I'd found myself with jungle time to spare so I investigated further. There was a young lady and a chap teaching a kick-boxing class when I poked my head in. I didn't leave it poked in long, as there was a young Afghan lad very efficiently kicking the shit out of some fast moving pads and more guys sparring and waiting for a go with the very sparse kit. To see young lads up early and doing something with their time was a positive start.

I headed from the dome to see Nasser, noticing as I picked my way through the closely packed shelters, how quiet it was. The incessant hammering and panicked voices from the chaotic move were gone. There was stillness throughout the Jungle; people were still in bed, safe and comfortable.

Nasser and I took tea with his friends. They told me it was bad times in the jungle. People are running out of savings, they are cold and hungry, getting ill and becoming more and more desperate. Right wing thugs are picking off refugees around the edges of the camp and handing out severe beatings. Suicide, depression, addiction and antisocial behaviour are increasing. People cannot live like this indefinitely, it's inhumane.

One of the older guys is in his 50's, he didn't speak English but clearly demanded a fatherly respect, as he scolded one of the youngsters for wearing his shoes and getting them muddy. I look at their shoes and all are in a bad state. I make a mental note to keep an eye out for some decent boots and enquire as to their sizes; all are around 42/43, like most residents.

After tea my phone rings and Tom has a build ready for me to help with in the Sudanese area, so I thank my hosts, accept one more biscuit and head off with my tools.

I stopped at the showers to drop off the drill battery charger and a backgammon board to my friend Amir. He looks tired and as we hug and he kisses my face firmly, I can feel he is thinner again, his clothes baggy as they hang off his large frame.

Amir repeats the current worries of the jungle. Warning me that it is no longer safe at night in The Jungle for me. There are small resident gangs causing trouble and I should be very careful in Calais and around The Jungle as helping the refugees makes you dangerous enemies. He sends me on my way with a Snickers and tells me to have a safe day doing good work.

I head off to the self-build site via the "Jungle Books" library, dropping off a load of kids books. The level of English reading amongst the children here is astounding and both fiction and non-fiction for all ages is always appreciated. There is a hunger amongst the children in the camp to learn. The parents there, most having been well-educated and successful in business themselves (hence affording to get to safety) try to ensure their youngsters learn and play like any other child where possible.

All week, I handed out tennis balls to various kids I met, a donation from a Harpenden sports shop. The excitement in their eyes is almost heart breaking. Something as simple as a ball will bring so much pleasure. They find plastic bags to wrap the balls tightly in and then tape them up so they last as long as possible in the filth and mud.

The first build consists of four shelters. I start working on one with a Belgian couple. They're very friendly and useful, but it is their first day in the jungle and they are shocked at the small, lightweight shelters we are building. Time, cost, space and sheer numbers mean that we have to be as efficient as possible with production and materials, and the shelters are surprisingly warm as I had found out for a brief few hours the night before.

Once we have the frame up, the Belgian couple help out on the others as two Sudanese guys who will be living in the shelter join me to clad and insulate. Manai and Manny were hard workers and took care in their work, with their big smiles as they quietly sing to themselves hammering clout nails through the tightly stretched plastic sheet. While they hammer I staple, much faster, but we don't have enough staplers. I leave Manny my stapler and run off to see Nasser. He has my stapler from last time I was here!

I find Nasser and he runs off to find it, returning a few minutes later looking rather ashamed. "I am so sorry my brother," he says, looking down as he hands me my stapler back. I'd only been away a week and it had gone from brand new to rusty and knackered in no time at all. It's impossible to keep anything dry in The Jungle and I should have expected it really.

"Another victim of The Jungle. May he rest in peace," I laughed. Nasser clearly relieved laughs with me.

I return with the knackered stapler and show Manai it's broken and take the rusty staples out. He grins and grabs it, going inside the shelter and touching it to Manny's backside, while making a "tck tck" noise with his teeth. Manny jumps a mile and Manai and I collapse over each other, hugging and laughing like silly schoolboys.

The workshop has run low on insulation so we are improvising with blankets, but they are also in short supply. I nip back to the horse van and grab a dozen blankets and sleeping bags I'd brought over, stuffing them in a bright pink granny trolley. There's enough to insulate all 4 shelters now and any extra is put on the ceiling to offer an extra barrier against the cold. After briefly mocking my pink trolley, Manny changes his mind when I offer it to him for transporting their water containers. His friends then, in turn, mock him before one of the ladies says it's very good and thanks me with a big thumbs up and a smile, putting it in her shelter.

We help finish up all the shelters, the stragglers quickly completed with a multitude of staplers and hammers now available. We tidy up and gather the tools. It's only about 4pm, but the light is already fading as we hand over padlocks and keys. There aren't enough materials for more shelters so we can head off after this and get tools ready for tomorrow.

Manai and Manny shake my hand and give me a hug. It had been a pleasure working with them. They thank me for all my help, and I thank them for theirs. Thanking them often confuses people. It's strange I guess, but despite the fact that they get a shelter out of it, I am still grateful to them. Not all residents help build and it's not always an enjoyable experience, but today had been good.

Maybe it's the polite Englishman in me, or maybe it's just that after working together and enjoying each other company creating something together, I can't help but say 'thank you'. Maybe I'm really thanking them for the experience, the chance to help, the human connection. Or maybe I'm just grateful that when I do this, there are moments when you feel there is nothing more important to be doing than helping someone build themselves a shelter. It is uplifting, knowing you're not on a commute to London, or drinking a Costa, or watching the TV. Knowing you are doing something that finally matters, not ignoring those nagging voices that say, "This is not OK. Do something." Voices I ignored for a long time at the detriment of my happiness and mental well-being.

⌘

It doesn't feel good in an egotistical way or arrogant sense of pride. There's no goal scoring high, or smug satisfaction but for me a Zen that calms the furious mind, a wave of peace, as the realisation that I am listening to my conscience and doing what little I can, to be the change I want to see.

⌘

As I drove out that evening across the wasteland, the oppressed residents on one side, the oppressors armed to the teeth on the other, I was given a sign of hope: Kids playing cricket and football out in the open space, a peaceful demonstration of humanity. It gave me images of soldiers downing weapons and playing football and singing Silent Night.

But that was probably all bollocks. I was tired and the Jungle plays with your perceptions. Realistically they're just children; no politics there. They just wanted to find somewhere flat to play, somewhere to forget, to pretend to be a professional footballer and run around with your arms high in celebration, to hit a six or bowl out a friend...to play, to just be children.

Waste not:

We had timber frames and plastic ready to go at the workshop, but a lack of pallets meant we were running out of floors. The van drivers were heading out to collect free pallets 200 miles away so there would be no self-builds today. The lack of insulation meant a call to a fellow charity, and a collection of blankets needed to be arranged, leaving the workshop quietly producing plastic sheets and doors.

My job for the day was to measure up and start making some shelving for a distribution hut in the Afghan area. One of the more challenging areas in which to distribute items to desperate, frustrated people.

I headed in with half a dozen sacks of firewood, some plastic roofs and spare lengths of 2"x2" pine. Everyone needs a roof or a couple of lengths of timber to reinforce their porch or make a table. Whilst the team can't build shelters, there's nothing holding back the industrious Jungle workers from making their lives more comfortable.

I headed to the "Kabul Cafe" where I needed to meet the leader of the Afghan "family" or "organisation" or whatever you might like to call them. I like to consider them community leaders doing a tough job. Anything beyond that is above my pay grade. As I spend my days saying over and over, "I am not the boss, I just build."

'Steve' the community leader isn't there. But as I turned up with about 50 DVDs for them, it wasn't long before I was having a hot tea and signing out the key. One of the guys came with me to make sure I was legit and keep an eye on the few items already in the distribution hut. Turning young lads away every few seconds and telling them, "No line. Tomorrow. Tomorrow, " clipping them round the ear when the over zealous or inquisitive few tried to come in and poke around.

No pressure then mate. I measured up as quickly as I could in a dark hut and sat in the van as I made a sketch. It was 7m long and 2.4m wide, lots of space for shelves at the back and a serving counter, which needed to stop people being able to reach the shelves, the volunteers or get access to them. Shouldn't be a problem. I dread to think what I might charge for a similar project made beautifully at home, but this will not be pretty. Function will far outweigh form.

Just having the horse van or probably any van in the jungle will attract attention and requests and by the time I'd gone back and forth to the restaurant and got everything done. I'd also given out five plastic sheets and a few dozen timbers. Not to mention the handfuls of nails we are constantly asked for. There is a recognised hand gesture for a nail. A person will put the end of their index finger across the other index finger making a "t" shape. The finger can then be moved up or down to signify the length of nail required. There are some very talented builders in the Jungle so they can be any size, but often it's little clout nails for securing plastic sheeting. The coastal wind in The Jungle can be icy cold and ferocious, and the noise of flapping plastic is a constant hum.

As I drive out I saw an Eritrean lady who wasn't wearing warm enough clothes for the cold day. My mother in law had donated a long fur coat that had been passed down but never really worn. Rather than throwing it in with all the other donations I had kept it in the van so climbed out and gave it out to her. Returning her smile and telling her to wear it and to, "Stay warm," using the international "stay warm" gesture and hugging myself whilst nodding like an idiot.

She thanked me and held my hand tightly for a moment and held eye contact. I could try and explain what I saw there; words like sadness, gratitude and pain, but it is almost impossible to explain the look in a Jungle residents eyes. Beat up, but not beaten.

We said goodbye and she thanked me again before running off into a shelter. As I drove away I heard a shout and saw a tall thin Eritrean man running out of the shelter. I slowed my crawl to a stop, as her husband caught up with me, hugged me through the open window and said in a lovely accent, "Thank you brother. Thank you man. Lovely coat. My wife is always cold. Thank you."

That was three of us already warmer as I headed back to the workshop to make some shelving.

I had hoped to use 2"x2" pine and sheet material to make the distribution units, but workshop karma was repaying me for the plastic and timber I'd handed out freely. Instead I'm asked to create the units out of some chipboard sheets with batons already pinned to them. There's about 4 pallets of the boards. Nobody has a clue what their original use would have been, but the chipboard can't be burnt or used. The yard managers want it out of the way. The workshop wants it out the way and it appears I am now the solution to making it somehow useful!

After a coffee, a smoke and some more time with the pencil, paper and calculator, I start cutting the sheets into shelf and side components. I'm using a table saw I donated on my last visit, with no guard on the blade and no cut out switch. It's about as far from Health and Safety standards as you could possibly get and few volunteers are even allowed near it. I entered the zone and got my head down. It's easy to work hard with volunteers all beavering away in their corners surrounding you.

Rolls of plastic are being cut to length ready for cladding. The last of the pallets are paired up or reconstructed and made into matching half floors, complete with a damp proof layer and 8' x 4' OSB sheet floor. Timbers are chopped to length using jigs and stored in their respective places. Shelter sides are built and stacked against the wall, the workshop gradually getting smaller as everyone does their part.

⌘

The previous night I'd been heading out for dinner when Boomer invited me to dinner at his caravan. Boomer is a hero, with long hair, a loud voice and razor sharp mind. He works like a man half his age, almost always knows best and will go out of his way to help. Time spent with Boomer is always good time so I joined him for a beautiful Ragu and some red wine, of course.

Over dinner I was introduced to the lovely Simone who helps run the kitchen, and Alfie her son. He's home schooled and has tried his hand at all sorts of jobs from sorting donations, kitchen work, distributions in The Jungle and so much more. If someone needs an extra hand with this or that he's happy to try something new. He speaks fluent French and had probably learnt more from volunteers, being there for a short time, than most kids had learnt in a year in school. My favourite thing about Alfie is he's always up to some sort of mischief, whether it's banging on a caravan in the morning, or locking someone in the loo. He finds fun everywhere and would often check whether what he was about to do would cross the line. I never had to say no, but then I was always unsure of where the line was.

Not every child is supposed to sit in a classroom, not every child learns best that way and for some, they are wasted years of lost opportunity. Alfie is being given the opportunity to reach his full potential by learning in a different environment and I applaud Simone for that and Alfie for embracing it...when he's not playing PlayStation.

Alfie arrives at the workshop and offers to help, but the only work I can give him is taking my scraps from by the saw and knocking the wood batons off the chipboard for kindling. He grabs a hammer and keeps at it for a few hours without complaint.

The workshop worked late, waiting for the drivers to return. By the end of the day I had all the components cut up ready and three units as a service counter with a door and bar top flap to allow access. It wasn't nearly done. 'Steve' the Afghan distribution hut and The Jungle residents who had been told 'tomorrow' would have to manage for another day. But tomorrow is a flexible term in The Jungle and is usually said with uncertainty, "Tomorrow?"

The pallet run guys returned, refreshed from a day of stress free driving. It had been like a day off for them, without people badgering them for shelters or navigating The Jungle to build sites. They'd listened to music, relaxed and returned jubilant. The mood was good as we unloaded the pallets and loaded the vans up for the builds the next day.

The positive vibe continued into the evening as we had a fire and workshop gathering, planned the days ahead, took the piss... and as always in these situations, a few ridiculously talented people shaming my total musical ineptitude with brilliant guitar skills and beautiful voices. It was a great end to the day and by the time I got to the shelter next to the workshop, I was too tired to worry about the cold much, as I 'snuggled in' under a dozen blankets with Phil and Tom my bed fellows for the week.

Distribution hut:

It was nice to have a job ready to crack on with first thing and with people waiting on my shelving I got stuck in.

At around 10am news hit the workshop that the French authorities would be bulldozing the church and any spare hands were being called to salvage what they could. I stayed at the workshop, alone.

Having seen the aftermath of bulldozers, I knew the reality was there would be little to salvage. Whilst the witnessing and recording of such an act should be done, it wasn't my place to do it. My skill set was more useful here. I took a moment in the now silent workshop and thought of all the residents that had found some strength or guidance through the church and acknowledged their loss. There was nothing more I could do.

By midday I was finished and loaded up the van with a little help from people popping in to ask me for various things. All of a sudden I was the workshop boss. I pretty much let people take what they needed; everyone had a story of hardship to go with their request.

Phil brought me lunch and gave me one of his almost too painful massages preparing me for a busy afternoon of construction.

After lunch, I passed off the responsibility of workshop guardian and headed into the Jungle with a few sacks of firewood and the shelving units.

After getting the key, I unloaded the tools. Fortunately, I could park right next to the hut, but with lots of people hovering around, checking out what was happening, keeping an eye on the tools whilst unloading was going to be a mission. I loaded the tools back into the front of the van and locked it. I took all the shelves and smaller components out of the van and started lining sections up in the hut. All the time having to tell inquisitive people, "No line. No line. I am building." It was painfully slow, but eventually I only had the big heavy sections left.

It was around then a young Afghan lad maybe 14 popped his head in, "Line?" he asked.

I sighed, it was getting tedious, "No line! I am building. No line, just me, building all this! Tomorrow. Tomorrow." He turned to go and then came back.

"I help?" he asked, my frustrations understood and his foreseeable calendar clear, I took a moment and accepted his offer, shaking hands. He introduced himself as Samir. He kept an eye on the hut, proudly telling people, "No line, today we build. Come back tomorrow."

I got the tools from the van and took them to back to the hut, before returning for the large units. The largest were too heavy for Samir and were on top of the counters, so I approached four Sudanese guys standing nearby. "Good morning brothers. How are you today?" I asked when they had finished speaking and turned their attention to me. "Can you help me with the distribution hut?" I said pointing at the full van and miming a lifting motion.

They smiled and nodded, "No problem, no problem."

We all unloaded the remaining bulk and crammed it into the hut. I grabbed the firewood from the van and locked it. Giving a few sacks to my Sudanese helpers and one to Samir with my thanks for their assistance.

It was about 2pm when I shut myself in the dark hut, I turned on the head torch and started to build.

⌘

I was pretty chuffed with my work, 5 columns of 3 rows of shelves ran along the back wall and along one end. The long deep counter joined to the front wall at both ends, allowed a few refugees through the door and in front of the counter, but stopped them being able to walk or reach around the sides. The bar flap and door were lockable from the inside giving the volunteers a physical barrier from which to work behind, allowing them to feel safe and in control and there was more shelving beneath the counter top. It was a job well done and all made from crap nobody wanted, which made it even better.

I tidied the tools, opened the door and realised it was night time again. I loaded the van, dropped the key to the Kabul Cafe and headed back to the workshop.

I arrived back to discover that there were new gas fuelled showers installed. Oh the little things! It probably wasn't 'the greatest shower I had ever had in my life ever. But it felt like it at the time. I finally got clean, washed the sawdust and grime off and put on clean clothes. It was wonderful.

Then despite being tired, I headed out for a hearty pub meal; knowing I was back on self-builds tomorrow and remembering various promises I had made, to look after myself as well as others.

After all, you never know what could happen tomorrow in the Jungle

Building shelters:

The first build was a heavy pre-clad shelter near the showers. We met Ben Harrison 'in the yellow jacket', a long term volunteer who works twelve hour days organising shelter distribution. His focus has always been on helping the most vulnerable first and slowly he has created success through sheer determination and hard work.

I'm often heard saying, "I'm not that Ben." What he has achieved, with the support of others is incredible and his calm nature and quietly spoken approach is the only way to deal with people in a desperate situation.

But he is also firm and didn't hesitate to tell a disgruntled group of young men who have been waiting a month, that there are some people who have been waiting in a tent for 3 months and they have to be patient. They will get a shelter.

I'm building with 'gap year' Tom and some young Afghan boys, hence the board cladding not plastic. The pre-fabs are quick and easy to assemble and it's only the insulation that takes time. It's cosy in the hut, stapling and tacking away with our head torches on. There was little joviality though. Whilst they were pleased to have the security and warmth of the shelter, I could see in their eyes they were tired of the damp, the mud, lining up for shoes, or food or a blanket. I couldn't blame them and we worked away together making the best of the situation.

After the usual Shokran (Thanks) and handshakes, Tom headed off to find the next build. Like some sort of wrong place, wrong time, work magnet, I had once again managed to find some extra jobs.

I popped to the tea hut, situated next to the dome; it's a frequent hangout of young teens who have quite literally got nothing at all to do. They hang out there drinking tea and creating minor mischief in order to catch the attention of the pretty tea girls.

The lock on the tea hut had been broken by a couple of lads after the girls had lost the key. It had apparently taken seven seconds. It was a quick fix, as was the latch and lock on their self-built compost toilet. It had been the victim of break-ins and protest poo's previously, but ladies who tea need their little privacies, so most residents respect their abode. The last touch was fixing a small pallet below the window. Only big enough for one person at a time, but enough to make eye contact and passing tea a little easier. It lasted a week before it was taken and used as firewood, I should have known better than to use anything you can burn!

⌘

Next job was over near the Church. The previous evening I had promised a lady I would return with a new roof. I recovered her roof with the help of her teen son in about twenty minutes and then we did their neighbours.

One of the heads of the Kurdish family came over and asked for some plastic and tools for a few more roofs and before I knew it the van was almost empty. I lent the Kurds a stapler. We were old acquaintances now and I knew I could get it back later, besides I had a spare, so I left them a load of staples and let them crack on.

Before I could leave I had to fix five locks for the Eritreans, who had come over to ask for a quick job: three latches on a group of four shelters used for sleeping and cooking and another two on their friends shelters.

I was given tea without milk or too much sugar, which was refreshing for a change and a small plate of rice and beans. They had seen me alone and busy and all wanted to say thank you. Even the ladies in the group (who often hide away, culturally shying away from the volunteers) poked their heads out of the homely shelter to say thank you for taking the time.

I gave them the last of my firewood from the van, there were only a few bits of plastic and a handful of long timbers left in there now. I'd better get back to work.

⌘

I headed off to meet the others for the next job, a group of self-builds. When I caught up they were still unloading, with a group of about six lads crowding round. I was immediately introduced to Tahir. He was sixteen and spoke very good English. It transpired that they had taken down their clad six man hut themselves during the move. They had carried it 500 metres over rough terrain and re-built it themselves with hammers and nails. But the roof was no longer waterproof and it was getting pretty bad inside. I left the self-build teams to it and went with Tahir and his friends. Tahir was outspoken and surly (understandably), but his friend Ahmed was a lovely guy:

athletic and good looking, with blue eyes and a, "Fuck it. Shit could be worse," grin.

They'd done a great job on the shelter, even adding a large veranda for cooking and drying clothes and shoes. Made from scavenged tree boughs and lashed together it looked reasonable. I gave it a good shake...it barely moved an inch. I looked at Ahmed and Tahir, who waited proudly for the verdict.

"Good?" Ahmed asked.

"No..." I paused for effect, "it's fucking good!" I grinned. He grinned back and Tahir finally loosened up a bit.

Complete with a 2m half-built veranda it needed 8m X 4m of plastic and there wasn't anything that size on camp. I gave the lads some timber to finish the veranda and some plastic for the sides and headed back to the workshop for the roof, with a promise to return as soon as I could.

By the time I had got to the workshop, cut the plastic and returned, it was getting dark. They had finished the extension and were looking tired. I was tired too, so when the discussion of tonight or the morning came up, I was fairly neutral but Tahir was resolute and rallied the other lads as Ahmed and I shared a wink and a hidden grin. The guy up on the roof and I grabbed a corner and let them take the lead, they'd managed up to now. It was windy and trying to hold down and fix an 8m X 4m plastic sheet is a bit like flying a giant kite whilst wielding a hammer and a nail. But eventually, between us we managed, and it was securely fastened with hospital corners and looking smart. We all agreed Tahir was right; tonight was better.

There was a happier mood amongst the group, their hard work finally done, their shelter dry and much more habitable. They were pleased with themselves and they had every right to be. They thanked me and offered to make tea, but it was already late and I needed sleep and maybe even food. We said our goodbyes, Tahir and I shook hands and I told him to keep being a good leader.

Ahmed gave me hug and another smile and said, "Today was a good day. Thank you, Ben." And that was enough for me.

Human connections:

I headed into the Jungle early with a familiar cargo of useful items. I hadn't seen much of the people I had met previously in the Kurdish area, having left them with tools and hardware. I knew they would have been proactive and I wanted to makes sure they had everything they needed. I also had a few items for some of the kids.

It was so early when I arrived at the Kurdish area that almost everyone was asleep. A young lad of maybe 9 years, was hanging about. We had met before, his name was Mo and he was a good boy, fast becoming a man. Always busy doing something useful. He helped his mother and the others nearby that needed it.

I gave him a tennis ball and asked if anyone else was awake. He introduced me to the little girl next door to him who had taught me some Arabic last time. "Toni," I said proudly, remembering the greeting.

"Hi," she replied, smiling. "How are you today?"

Impressed as ever with her perfect English, I gave her some books and a ball and she said thank you and ran off to show her mother.

Mo took me to meet his family, a mother and little sister. I had some scarves, hats and gloves as well as books and sweets, which I shared with them. As we sipped tea and watched Mo read to his sister, their mother nodded her thanks and used a circular motion of her hand to show she understood that they were to be shared with her neighbours and passed around the kids. Amongst others, there were some Dr Seuss books and the boy looked up smiled and gave me a little thumbs up.

I was just leaving, when their neighbour asked me for a moment of my time. We had met before too, when I had fixed a roof for him, but today it was a latch. He was in his late forties, had a grasp of English, a round build, and a greying beard. He was always friendly and had a lovely wife and four children: two boys around eleven and nine and a little girl and boy, both under three. Whilst I was fixing the latch, the toddlers would run up to the door laughing at me before running away again. As with most youngsters, this was their time of day and they were full of energy and fun. They were all smiles and giggles. It was adorable and we had a lovely game of peekaboo while I made their lock as secure as possible.

Their eldest son was wrapped up under a blanket in the corner and his dad asked me to come in and have a look at him.

"I am not doctor. No medicines," I explained but went in and had a chat with him about his symptoms, whilst his mother shared some eggs onto a plate and pressed a fork into my hand and gestured me to sit with a firm hand on my shoulder. I sat on the floor, the toddlers wriggling their bottoms next to me and watching me eat.

The son had a mild case of man flu by my expert diagnosis. Normally I'd prescribe a half pint of "man the fuck up" but instead, I told him to rest and got some tins of fruit I had in the van and gave them to his mother. I didn't have much else. What he really wanted was Vapour-rub and his Dad showed me the empty pot and pleaded with me to get some more if I could. I promised to try and put the empty pot on the dashboard and made a mental note to find a pharmacy before tomorrow.

I had another self-build with Tom next. He had already found the location, unloaded the bits and secured the flattest ground to build on, so it was a pretty straightforward operation and before we knew it, we were done and it was nearly lunchtime.

I had a 1 tonne grab bag of kindling in the van, which we managed to dump in the family area without anyone noticing, making it a lot less stressful than a distribution.

Our afternoon was looking fairly free and I was planning on filling it with some chicken and chips from the Afghan Flag restaurant. But sadly this was not meant to be.

⌘

The self-builds were grinding to a halt again, as we were all out of insulation. Tom and I changed our lunch plans and headed to the Brico to buy some insulation rolls. Brico is pretty much a French B&Q, which as such closes for a 3 hour lunch, of course.

We went back to the workshop and managed to grab lunch, (vegan curry again) from the kitchen. We waited for the Brico to open and bought £600 worth of insulation, enough to last this afternoon and tomorrow morning, but not much beyond that.

A lot of the volunteers were taking the afternoon off to see the Royal Shakespeare Co. perform Hamlet at the Dome. I wouldn't be going for various reasons:

a. It was put on for the refugees and long-term volunteers as a cultural event to break the monotony. I am only here for a week or so at a time and I am here to work. There isn't time for me to get bored.

b. Hamlet is in my humble opinion, average. I prefer A midsummer nights dream. I was very pleased to pass by though and see lots of refugees standing on huts, vehicles and crowding around to see what for many was probably their first, live experience of Shakespeare.

Most of the volunteers lasted 10 minutes, before realising I was right and Shakespeare's still less fun than working for free.

⌘

Tom and I headed off to find Pete the driver; the stuff of legend. Pete has an impossible task of dropping buildings whilst trying to explain that he's not got spare shelter components on board or can't get them a shelter.

"You must speak to Ben or Liv," I hear as I approach.

"Ben with the yellow jacket," I reiterate as I approach, wondering if Ben might one day rock up in a red coat and have a day off from the insanity throwing the whole system into chaos. The anarchist in me likes that idea but sadly he's indispensable.

Whilst we unload the van, I catch the end of a conversation. Some Sudanese guys keep pestering Pete for the use of his van. While Pete patiently explains he has two more houses to unload after this one and then has to return to the workshop, "I am sorry my friend I cannot help," he says finally.

They throw their hands up in frustration and start to walk away.

I asked Pete what they needed. They had some heavy pallet floors to move to the other side of the jungle. It would take hours of carrying them between them and lots of runs on back and forth; or one trip in the horse van. Pete and the others had the self-builds under control so I offered my services.

"I can help," I said as Pete smiled and shot me a look that said, "When can't you?"

They turned back, the relief plain on their faces.

"Yes brother, come, come. Thank you brother."

We all jumped into the van, Bob Marley was singing redemption song on the CD player and we had a little vocal performance as we made our way, me and two guys in the front and another four or five standing in the back looking after my tools. We bumped our way through the Jungle, one of my passengers leaning out the window, laughing and telling friends he passed about their luck.

We arrived to collect the four heavy sections of floor. I wasn't allowed to do any heavy lifting as I was apparently doing enough. So I waited in the sun and chatted to a shopkeeper whilst I waited for them to return.

The floors at 2.5m long and 1.2m wide, were a big lump but we managed to load them all in the van and twenty minutes later we were Jammin' our way back across The Jungle with Sudanese song coming from the excited voices in the back of the van. It probably only took an hour total, to do what would have taken seven of them all day. Once we had unloaded and the thanks were done with, their infectious positivity had re-energised me for the final self-build of the day.

The others were well underway and we efficiently worked our way through the straightforward build. The Iranian lads we built with were enthusiastic too, which was lucky as it was already getting dark, and at twice their age I was beginning to feel familiar aches in my neck, back and shoulders, but we got it done.

It was late when I left the Jungle, maybe 9pm. I was alone in the van on a quiet stretch of track when I saw 4 teens approaching as I slowly drove past. I always have my window rolled all the way down. I see some people come in with their windows rolled up and their doors locked...I'm not sure how they expect to shake someone's hand or say good morning to a brother or sister though a locked door, but in this case it might have been prudent.

Whilst one went to the passenger side, two went to the back door and the other came to the window. All smiles and, 'Hello brother how are you,' but for the first time in The Jungle it didn't feel right. I couldn't see his right hand, down by his side. I kept the van rolling on slowly.

"Stop my friend, no problem, no problem," he promised at the window. I didn't want to offend, but it didn't feel right, so I went with my instincts and got out of there, accelerating away as he shouted

angrily after me. A long day in the jungle, tired and hungry, maybe I was overreacting.

But I'm rarely spooked and hindsight is a wonderful thing when you've just been shanked. Better safe than sorry.

Mrs Ali:

I left the workshop, tooled up, loaded with timber and plastic and headed to the Jungle The small empty tub on the dashboard reminding me to make a small detour en route to a pharmacy. I picked up a pot of Vapour-rub for the Kurdish boy with man-flu I'd met the day before and went straight to his family's shelter. They were very happy to see me and wanted to make me breakfast, but I had promised to be elsewhere first thing so had to politely decline. I stayed for a quick tea, playing peekaboo with the two little ones whilst it finished brewing. Mother did what mothers do and fussed over her boy, whilst he protested that he could do it himself.

I chatted with the father and he told me a familiar story of violence at home; the loss of his brother and parents finally pushed him to fearing home more than a long dangerous journey with his family. But now he was here, there was nowhere else to go. He wants the same thing any husband and father wants: safety, security, education and a chance for a life without fear of violence.

The Jungle was barely better than the bombs and terror at home, with fascist attacks and uncaring authorities regularly infringing on their human rights, little education and a future unknown.

⌘

After tea, warm hugs and thanks were given, the father walked out to the van with me. He shook my hand and hugged me again firmly, tears in his eyes; a proud man who was desperately trying to take care of his family with no resources. The Vapour-rub was a tiny gesture, but had made a difference to his family and his worries on that morning at least.

As I jumped in the van, Mo their young neighbour, ran out waving to me. "Sweets?" he grinned optimistically. I didn't have any more sweets, but had about five packets of airwaves chewing gum and offered him a packet. "Kaugummi!" he smiled and thanked me, before running back off to his shelter.

We were still low on volunteers so I was working alone again. Today's job was to put a roof over two caravans in the family area. The Iranian neighbours got on well and looked out for each other; a cover between their vans would allow them to dry wet clothes and keep the caravans cleaner inside.

As I carried the timbers and plastic over and got the tools together, the noise must have woken them and Ali poked his head out, checking I wasn't someone up to mischief. We'd met briefly the day before and he sleepily smiled and said Salam.

I gave them ten minutes to wake up a bit, allowing Ali's wife to pop out to a friend's and leave the men to it. Ali's wife was beautiful, olive skin and blue eyes, with a perfect smile. But as she left, a few instructions were given and I could see Ali and I had something in common; she was the boss.

Whilst Ali made us eggs with flat-bread for breakfast, I got started on the pine framework. It would have sides fixed to the caravans, a back wall and eventually a roof. I had made some progress when Ali called me in to eat.

We sat in the cramped, but warm van, their worldly belongings filling much of the space; Ali and I squeezed either side of the little table and shared a plate. Ali's English was good and as we scooped the delicious eggs up with the bread and chatted, he told me his story. His mother and father were Muslim, but growing up he had decided he wanted to be a Christian. A dangerous choice in northern Iran. His parents were not happy, but accepted his choice. Eventually though the Taliban had found out and had threatened to kill him and his wife. He mimed a hangman's noose. "And so we had to leave our home," he said with sadness.

In my trips to The Jungle I have probably met and talked to over a hundred people; all of them have a reason for leaving home. Different stories of fear and violence forced them from the country they grew up in and loved, bombs destroying whole towns and bullets mowing down friends. The Taliban, terrorists, ISIS, American or Russians.

Not a single one...not a single person in that camp has ever mentioned benefits. They want a chance to live and to work hard. If you think they are coming here to claim money off our government or steal your job, then I suggest you stop watching so much TV, take your head out of the sand, put down the propaganda newspaper and WAKE THE F**K UP!!

Ali and I continued with the shelter after breakfast and a few of his neighbours started waking up and saying hello. At least four people came up to me that morning and shook my hand saying I was doing a good thing and that Ali was a good, good man. It seems he had been looking after more people than just his next door neighbours.

By lunchtime, we managed to get the framework finished and the plastic cladding on the back wall, one of Ali's neighbours joining us in the build, another regularly bringing us hot tea.

Ali's wife returned with her friend and some chicken and rice for our lunch. She smiled at me and said it looked very good, before an exchange of words with Ali in a language I didn't speak but a tone I understood perfectly. He was being given instructions. We ate together again and Ali asked me if it was possible to put a front wall on the open porch area. His wife had said she needed a front to stop the wind and rain coming in. I had enough timber and plastic to do it, but was supposed to be making a wooden porch for a distribution hut later, so time was a factor. Each Jungle job you do needs to be time efficient as there are so many people who need help, but if you are going to help someone, you may as well improve their situation to the best of your ability, rather than do half a job and rush off. I agreed to put a front wall on too. Ali smiled, knowing his wife would be pleased.

After lunch we got the roof on, Ali and I each on a caravan roof, nailing and stapling the plastic to the timbers spanned across. Once done it would give them a 3.5m x 3.5m space. I popped to the van for some extra timbers and some plastic for the front wall and another neighbours roof. The neighbour borrowed a hammer and nails and sorted it himself with his young teenage son. While Ali and I started the framework for the front. Ali's wife returned, very happy with my efforts but another set of instructions for him. Ali looked at me apologetically and I knew there was another request.

"Mrs Ali, says please, she needs a door, to make us safe...and a table for outside." Ali said sheepishly. The job had almost gone from a tarpaulin roof to an entire shelter and now furniture!!

"I don't have a door, I'm sorry. But I can give you timber and tools to make a table." I offered.

"If I can get a door, will you fix it for us? Please, my wife is Mafia," he joked, I think.

I laughed, as it seems a beautiful woman with a strong mind gets what she wants, even in The Jungle. I agreed to fit a door if he could find one. I knew there weren't any unallocated ones in the vans, so it wasn't likely. Less than five minutes later Ali returned with a door, maybe his wife was Mafia!!

I fitted the door and finished the front wall, whilst Ali cut up some timbers for the table. His neighbours were right, Ali was a good man. As I was tidying up the tools, Mrs Ali returned and I gave her a padlock for the door. She beamed at me, squeezed both my hands and said in broken English, "Very thank you, good, good job."

I smiled and thanked her then held my hands up and told her Ali did most of it. She understood and we all laughed, but he proudly showed Mrs Ali her new table and she gave him a big hug. The morning job had turned into an all day mission. Various neighbours had used any spare timber and plastic and it was already getting darker.

One of their neighbours had asked me to get some sealant for his caravan which was leaking. He was an elderly man; the oldest I have seen in The Jungle, maybe in his eighties. I'd brought him food before and we always nod in passing, sometimes shaking our heads and saying about The Jungle, "...no good, no good." I knocked on his door, wished him a good night and promised to come tomorrow morning. Three people had promised him now that they would come tomorrow, but they had never showed up, possibly distracted by other larger jobs or situations.

He nodded and said, "You are a good boy, I will see you tomorrow."

I got back to the van to find a group of young lads hanging around, looking for some mischief to break up the boredom. One of the lads asked for money and I said I didn't have any. He didn't seem convinced and looked a little angry. I did have some chocolate though and handed out a dozen snickers and lion bars. A couple of lads snatched two without thanks. I told them off and made them give the extras to other boys.

One of the older lads became slightly aggressive, pointing a can of black spray paint right in front of my face, moving it closer to my eye. He was testing me. I hoped. A tactic often seen in The Jungle to test your mettle and determine whether you are worth their time; if you lose your temper or show fear, you lose their respect and possibly the sight in one eye.

I gave him the sort of look I save for my daughter. The one I use when in public, when whatever she's doing needs to stop instantly, without any discussion. A look that requires no words and simply says, "You can continue in this direction if you like, but I really wouldn't if I were you." He got the message, respect was earned and he slunk off.

A younger boy had said, no thank you to chocolate, but now pointed to a banana on the dashboard. I smiled, and gave him the banana and a packet with three pots of mixed fruit salads in. He was very grateful and hid them away in his coat, thanking me. I was just happy to see a youngster refusing the sugary treats and opting for the healthy fruit.

A Sudanese man lived near where the van was parked. I often give him firewood. He has a sheltered seating area for people to join him around his fire, and the range of nationalities there was always varied and changing, so I help him help others. In return I know he keeps an eye on the van and shoos away some of the troubled teens. He told me a small boy was looking for me and had been over three times today; he wanted sweets. I thanked him and guessed it was probably Mo.

As I was driving out, I passed Mo. The young Kurd shouted and ran up to the van again. He had been looking for me. "Do you have more Kaugummi?" he asked. "I love this!!" He held up a nearly empty packet of airwaves.

I gave him another packet and told him, not to eat too many before dinner. He promised and ran off again, a big smile on his face. I drove out of The Jungle, a tired smile on mine. Feeling pretty content with my days work.

Homeward bound:

I arrived in The Jungle early. Most residents were still asleep, so I drove as quietly as possible to the dome and parked up.

I had a caravan to seal and people to say goodbye to, but should have plenty of time. The Euro-tunnel home was around 2pm but there were other volunteers to round up for a ride home, one of whom needed to make a Gatwick flight.

Ryan was flying back to Scotland after over four months living in a freezing caravan next to the dome. He had been fixing structures and situations in the Jungle for longer than most and had a great relationship with the people there.

I popped in for a cuppa to warm me up before starting work. While we were discussing the days exit strategy, a friend of Ryan's arrived handing him back a hammer, while rolling a smoke in his left hand, and immediately then shaking mine with the other and introducing himself. Let's call him, 'Hammer-man'.

Hammer-man used to have a small Jungle restaurant. He had managed to build it over time, since his arrival. He used to be an interpreter for the American Army in Afghanistan, but was abandoned to run for his life when they left the country and the Taliban regained control. Knowing that the American connection was less helpful than a British forces connection (still generally ignored) he had put what he had into the enterprise, looking at the long term possibility of needing an income whilst waiting and hoping.

Sadly, the French authorities had destroyed his restaurant, along with other parts of The Jungle. It was where he and his friends had also slept and socialised, but Ryan had helped settle them into a cold, leaky caravan near his and together they had fixed them up as best they could, and made them comfortable. He also helped fix situations in The Jungle and was very useful for clear communication. Subsequently, any friend of Ryan was a friend of his.

Hammer-man, asked me if the horse van was mine, I explained a friend was loaning it to me.

"But you are always driving it?" he asked. He had seen it a lot in the Jungle, here and then gone and then back again, all over the site. He thanked me for the work I was doing for all the jungle. It was nice to know that my efforts to help in every community had not only been noticed, but were appreciated. Hammer-man not only considered himself a proud Afghan but a member of a wider community too.

⌘

When your back's are against the wall, I guess you have to stand together.

⌘

We discussed family and sport and then why so many British people are helping in the Jungle, but Britain won't let them in. It was a strange mix of chat and Jungle politics. As we said goodbye, he told me I was welcome to stay in his caravan anytime as I came to the Jungle to help others, but to bring warm clothes...and if possible a large boat. We'd only just met but I had been offered shelter, should I need it. You don't find that very much in England.

I headed off to the old man's caravan. There was no sound or movement inside, so I quietly went about my business. As I stretched for all the high points and found every joint and seam, I thought I was quiet as a ninja, but it appeared not. I was about halfway through, when a cup of tea in a strong, wrinkled hand came through the door, followed by a brown face, framed in white hair with bright smiling eyes and a big smile.

He stepped back and saw the thick bead of sealant that now waterproofed the roof, windows, door-frame and more. He clapped me on the shoulder and said, "Good boy, you are good boy," before pointing at the next bits to do. We nodded back and forth, as I sipped tea. Not allowed to put it down to cool, I took the break and we walked round his caravan discussing where it might be leaking.

After tea, he returned to the warm and I carried on. The sealant, lasting just enough to do all the necessary parts of the caravan.

I nipped back to the van to clean the sealant off my fingers and returned with a bag containing tuna, baby wipes and a child carry pack that we had used when Layla was 3-4 years old. The family next door, had a toddler of that age and the parents knew that there may be more walking in their future. The Jungle is an uncertain place. Wipes are great for everyone in the jungle and you can never have too many young or old! The old man thanked me for coming back and fixing his van and gratefully accepted the cans of tuna and some wipes. I promised to return again soon and told him to take care.

I returned to the van to find two pensive faces. One is the Afghan lad who had pointed a can of spray paint at my eye and the other is Nasser. I let the lad speak first. He apologises for yesterday's trouble, said that he understands I am just here to help and thank you but he was angry and hates The Jungle.

I tell him I understand and that it's OK. He nods and disappears off, probably to Hammer-man, to tell him he has apologised. I can't even remember mentioning it to anyone, but must have said something to Ryan I guess.

Nasser, has the puppy dog eyes on again and I know what's coming. We chat as we head toward his shelter. "Please, you are going today. Take me with you Benedict's," he begs. Leave the back open and I will hide...".

"They will find you brother," I warn him. "They look every time. There is no chance."

They do search the van, inside and out, every time I return to the UK. They would find him, and then send him back to The Jungle, via a beating and detention camp with a black mark against his name and future asylum applications. And I'd get to see the inside of a cell no doubt. There has to be a better way than joining the smugglers!! Although writing to my local MP has done little so far.

Eventually, I manage to convince Nasser it's not a good idea and we say our goodbyes. I give him a little money to help out with food. He initially tries to say no, but doesn't protest much. We both know he needs it. We hug and I tell him to keep hope.

He says that I am his only hope, and I walk back to the van feeling like shit, but knowing I was making the right choice.

I see Pete the driver of one of the self-build vans, and a key part of the build team, and pop over to say goodbye.

You'd think it was my first day in the jungle! Pete, is dropping a shelter to a group of Afghans, who said they could build. All other builders are busy and it now transpires, they can't build and were possibly just saying that to get a shelter quicker. I know, shocking!

They'll be buying a shelter next to the school next for the catchment area, or going to the church.

The tools were in the van, batteries were charged and I still had about an hour so I agreed to start the build, but me and my tools would be leaving soon. So it had to be a team effort.

We cracked on, levelling the floor and screwing it together, getting the frames on, cross braces, roof and door. I gave one of them my drill to use and the others hammers and saws and suddenly they were perfectly capable. By the time I had to leave, we had built a fast paced, efficient team. The plastic cladding was on and a couple of the taller guys were doing the roof. I gave them further instructions and they thanked me for my time, I left them hammers, nails and a couple of Stanley knives. All they would need to finish the insulation inside plus the all-important padlock.

Quick goodbyes, and half-jokes of, "See you in England. Inshallah," as the handshakes and hugs went round, before I grabbed the tools and rushed off to the van, no longer with "plenty of time."

At the van I did my usual quick clear out of anything "jungletastic" (greatly appreciated in the jungle): some bags of firewood, 2"x2" timbers, rest of my nails, a saw and some fruit and tuna and the last of the wipes. No line or ordered distribution. Just, to who's nearby, "Here have some firewood," which everyone needs.

"Excuse me, do you need a saw?"

Sometimes they say, "No, thank you. I am OK. I have a hammer, or food," allowing someone else in the community who needs it more to benefit.

The Jungle is a hive of industrious ingenuity; I can guarantee someone will make use of every last nail there. A use is even found for bottle tops, used as washers on tarpaulin and insulation, to broken bicycle's turned into water carriages.

Another panic jungle exit, I shouldn't expect anything else. There is always something to do in The Jungle. I gathered my travel companions and headed for the train, crossing the no-man's-land, towards the bridge and smiling at the cricket matches. Finally believing the volunteers had achieved the impossible: sheltered the vulnerable; moved the Jungle; fed the hungry; clothed the cold and finally, finally, got all but the last few out of tents and into shelters.

The residents had built their own communities in the wastelands of Calais. They had made efforts to put aside differences and live together in peace. They had chosen to hope and wait, on the freezing coastline of France, with no way to return home. That chance lost to persecution, war and terrorism. Family behind or ahead, they were now left with the Jungle and they made the best of it.

There was singing and laughing, children played, went to school, had friends and people who cared, looking after them. People sat around fires talking and welcoming those around them with cups of tea and food. There was hope.

Addendum:

A few weeks later, the French authorities ruled that the southern section of the Jungle could be cleared and the people there displaced once more. They would start with the South and will clear the homes of 3,500 people. And then, they may clear the north, displacing these communities and vulnerable minors again. They can either move as groups, into large cold tents, cooking outside on a fire, when they are lucky enough to have wood, living in conditions worse than prison camps, for an indefinite amount of time. Or some, can sleep in the shipping containers with biometric registration, no running water or amenities, merely a bed in a metal box, somewhere to sleep for the night, before going back out to the mud, to find a fire to stay warm and conversation to pass the time. One thing is sure, they cannot go back.

⌘

Thank you all for reading. I hope my words have painted a picture of the truth of the Calais jungle. There are many negative reports in the press, which is tied to the government and determined to cast refugees in a negative light. There is a humanitarian crisis on our doorstep. The residents of the Jungle are people like you and me. Some good, some bad, but mainly they're just people, waiting in desperation for a chance to have a life back. A life lost to violence and destruction, domestic unrest and foreign politics, all out of their control.

⌘

The politics and future, is a subject for someone else to write about. I wrote about this, to tell the story of the people I met in the Jungle: the kind and generous human beings, who are living thirty miles from our coast in hellish squalor. I feel I now have done that to the best of my ability and will continue to contribute to the work in Calais and being done by incredible volunteers everywhere. Any and all money made from my ramblings will also go directly to helping our displaced brothers and sisters.

The refugees future and the future of Europe is now more uncertain than ever. As I write this, the refugees have started to be evicted with force, including the use of batons, tear-gas and rubber bullets, with no discretion or harbour given to women and children, and belongings destroyed with their shelters. It's simply inhumane.

Whilst the authorities use force, the jungle children offer flowers, the Sudanese make the police who are destroying their shelters cups of tea and the peaceful protests and hunger strikes begin. If you can help as a volunteer please do. While it is sometimes demanding, you will never regret it. If you have already donated money or clothes, thank you from myself and the refugees, many of who have asked me to thank the people of the UK for all their help and compassion. They are aware their survival is only down to your collective kindness.

If all you can do is share the truth. That is enough.

Thanks again. Peace, love and unity.

Benedict O'Boyle

"Together we are change"

⌘

All proceeds from this book will be donated to the charities involved in supporting those working in the Calais Jungle - if you would like to donate further please do so through my gofundme campaign link -- go to gofundme.com/3ugq28hw

If you would like to get involved check out the following on Facebook

- Help Refugees - Calais, Europe and beyond
- L'auberge des migrants - Calais and Dunkirk refugees

About the Author

I'm told people like to know a bit more about the author. While this book probably shows the best of me, I am just another hopeless human, wandering and wondering through this life, doing my best, to do my best. I am not special, I am flawed and damaged like you, sometimes angry, sad, lonely or afraid. I am human.

I was born in West Sussex in the early eighties, both my parents were primary school teachers. In the early nineties, my parents moved my two sisters, my brother and I to Cyprus. My parents taught in the Armed Forces school there and for 8 years we lived in paradise away from much of the darkness and cruelty of the world. Cypriots are some of the kindest people I have ever met, always smiling, friendly and relaxed. We were made welcome wherever we went, invited to weddings of people we had never met, taken out to dinner to meet the whole four generations of family, dragged to village houses by strangers for Greek bread and village salad, people with little, sharing it and their company with us and teaching me love for all people, without me even realising it.

Using the location to travel around Cyprus, Jordan, Egypt, Israel and later beyond, I was shown that regardless of nationality, creed or colour, almost without exception, people are peaceful, kind and good hearted. When I see the broken faces of refugees carrying their children, I see the fathers who made my father and his family feel safe and welcome. I see the children I played with in the village squares or on the beaches. I see the tailor who made my fathers shirts, or secretary who worked at the school. I see people. Hungry, cold, scared people.

⌘

I returned to "normal society" in the UK for A-levels, before taking a gap year to travel independently before returning to University.

⌘

In 2005 I met my wife and graduated from Buckinghamshire Chilterns University. With a BA Hons in Furniture design and

Craftsmanship and a box of hand tools I started Benedict's Fine Furniture.

⌘

I have been a husband, a father and a bespoke furniture maker for a decade now. I have a beautiful daughter, Layla, who we took backpacking for 8 months, when she was three years old, we travelled overland through Africa, Asia and Australia. My book following our experiences, Little steps around the world, sold 500 copies and was written to encourage others to follow their hearts and take their kids backpacking.

Layla has also been to the Jungle to build shelters and hopes to return again soon.

⌘

I have amazing wife, Anya who supports me in my various endeavours and puts up with my many faults.

⌘

I currently divide my time between designing and making bespoke high quality furniture in Wheathampstead, Hertfordshire. Spending time with friends and loved ones in the UK and helping my brothers and sisters when and where I can in Calais.